MOSAICS

MOSAICS

general editor: Carlo Bertelli

Xavier Barral i Altet
Carlo Bertelli
Maria Grazia Branchetti
Per Jonas Nordhagen
Agnoldomenico Pica

GALLERY BOOKS
An Imprint of W. H. Smith Publishers Inc.
112 Madison Avenue
New York City 10016

Contents

Introduction

Mosaics are a familiar sight everywhere, in pedestrian underpasses, at airports, in hospitals and swimming pools. It would seem that mosaic, nowadays so widespread and almost mass-produced, is no longer considered as valuable and unique as it was for several thousand years. Sometimes certain artists, of their own accord or commissioned by art schools or industries, will try to recover old manual skills, and use them in an attempt to achieve lost expressive qualities. Even the more mundane mosaics that have been absorbed into the industrial world preserve some aspects typical of their long history, which we here show to have been much more varied than often imagined.

To grasp the intrinsic features of even the most ordinary mosaic of today, we must turn to what Le Corbusier, a pioneer of modern architecture, said in 1911 during a voyage of exploration through the art schools of Europe as far as Istanbul and Greece. While standing in the nave of St Demetrius in Salonika, holding a sketchbook with black cover in his left hand, the future architect wrote: "White/ grey/it is above all marble/grey, yellowish/lemon/,greenish/pinkish. Points/black marble/grey dark grounds on bright./The lesson of the mosaics in St Demetrius, Salonika is that/mosaic must achieve its effect/not by the colour but/by its material. That is why/ these almost white mosaics/are admirable and would be/modern improving on/those at Kahrie Djami which are/dead and unrepeatable." A subjective and unequivocal judgement which observes that one cannot follow the designs of the masterpieces of mosaic culture (those mosaics are dead and unrepeatable like ancient Greek culture is dead and unrepeatable). At the same time he is gathering hints from the poorer mosaics of Salonika beyond their formal features, in the search for some essential understanding, which he sees lying in the actual materials used. For Le Corbusier the ideal material is above all unworked stone and marble, rather than gilded or artificially painted tesserae. He also regards other aspects such as the brilliance and evenness of surface as vitally important. Both these features enable a certain type of architecture to "negate" the walls. As we shall see, architects and mosaicists were aware of this in the past, regarding mosaic as a source of reflected light which is tenuous and devoid of heaviness, solidity and definition. Without any other direct insight, Gaudí's white vaults under the terrace in Güell park, Barcelona catch and redirect light like the small vaults clad in white mosaic in the darkest corners of Fetiye Cami.

However, although architectural mosaic belongs ultimately to Mediterranean culture, twentieth-century work derives from other sources, too. Gaudí's spires and chimneys give us a first example of mosaic applied to three-dimensional elements. The effect is of great sculptured totem poles of Canadian Indians adapted to Mediterranean light or fused with the giddy pinnacles of Bangkok temples, where the sun and nocturnal lights raise brilliance from the fragments of porcelain tiles that cover them. Gaudí thus breaks the boundaries of Eurocentric vision. It is in Aztec culture that we occasionally find three-dimensional objects, masks or skulls clad in hard stone mosaic. Unlike the outlook of Asia and Europe, which turns nature into matter, here the materials of the object retain all their magic force.

It is this initial and invincible diversity which has given an unconscious academic stamp to the gallant attempts at expressing Mexican epic in mosaic in so many twentieth-century compositions. Nothing more clearly shows the contrast between the Old World *and the New than a small tableau by the famous anatomist Marcello Malpighi (1627–1694) in which a chessboard of different colours and veins is achieved with anatomical sections. Here nature indeed loses its proper role to become mere vision and show.*

The studies in this book show that mosaic art flows through history like a great river through a porous desert, disappearing and reappearing again. When mosaic became rare, Constantinople preserved a monopoly of it. Recent research shows that not even the iconoclastic crisis could interrupt this activity, lasting almost without break from antiquity to the fourteenth century. In this way mosaic was bound to be largely identified with the course of Byzantine art. Only in the field of floor mosaics could the West freely assert its inventiveness. In this volume that aspect is treated by a specialist, Xavier Barral i Altet, in a chapter on Western medieval and Islamic wall and floor mosaic. Likewise, eighteenth-century miniature mosaics and mosaic in general are for the first time viewed in an overall historical setting by a specialist, Maria Grazia Branchetti. Finally, Per Jonas Nordhagen has for decades studied Byzantine mosaic at first hand; Agnoldomenico Pica, historian and architect, has studied many of the mosaics he describes in situ. For my part, I am deeply thankful for what I have learnt from the teaching of Giovanni Becatti and from the practice of expert archaeologists like Lucia Guerrini, Ida Baldassare, Maria Luisa Matino Morricone and Luigi Rocchetti. For Renaissance mosaic my gratitude goes to Giuseppe Fiocco for his invaluable help, to André Chastel and to my friend Michelangelo Muraro.

Carlo Bertelli

ANCIENT MOSAICS

Most readers of an illustrated book on mosaics such as this one will have seen at least some examples of mosaic at firsthand and have some idea of what they are. Even the finest of photographers cannot evoke the personal relationship between a spectator and a mosaic. A mosaic floor, for instance, will never be seen in real life at the precise ninety-degree angle which a full photograph must reproduce. Many mosaics cover a very large area and it is necessary to walk on them, not only to discern every last detail but also to appreciate their general effect in particular settings. With wall mosaics, the way in which light is refracted and reflected off the individual cubes within the composition changes incessantly as the spectator moves around, especially when gold and silver fragments are used instead of marble, or coloured stone.

Wall mosaics are like a cloak over architectural arrangements, softening sharp edges and masking their solidity with reflected light. When the technique was in its infancy these characteristics presented craftsmen with a great many problems. The mosaics had to be delineated by a well defined framework so that the gleams and flashes of reflected light did not detract from the ordered architectural arrangement. This solution was often adopted in mosaics that decorated nineteenth-century buildings in somewhat eclectic styles, but even in very early examples, such as those in the nymphaea (niches dedicated to the nymphs and Muses) at Pompeii, areas of tessellation were enclosed in shell borders. These mosaics have been catalogued by D. Joly and one definite feature emerges from his work: these small mosaic-covered shrines with a fountain were sited in very small gardens, little more than courtyards, where the function of the mosaic was to belie the restricted space. In fact the earliest wall mosaics we know of are those in the extraordinary palace of illusion which Nero created in his magnificent Domus Aurea in Rome. The much later mosaics in the Galla Placidia Mausoleum in Ravenna show how important mosaic had become when it was a question of enriching and adding meaning to an architectural style which had not given consideration to the definition of areas. While the fountains of Pompeii exploited the mutually complementary effect of mosaic's sparkling lights and falling water, there were other very practical reasons for this juxtaposition. One of the oldest extant documents on mosaic is a papyrus fragment from 256–246 B.C., giving instructions for laying mosaic on the floor of a bath. Mosaics are even known to have been used in ships. Also in the mid third century B.C. (246–238), we know that Hiero II of Syracuse sent his own ship *Syracusia* to Alexandria for grain after drought had led to a poor harvest. The vessel excited great admiration for some of its cabins were floored with mosaic scenes from the *Iliad*. Suetonius tells us that Caesar even took slabs of mosaic on his campaigns, probably to ensure that the floor of his tent was not only elegant and impressive but also more hygienic than the more usual carpets or animal skins.

The mosaics used by Caesar must have been quite small and would have taken the form of a picture or *emblema*, as they were later to be known. Although decorative mosaic squares such as these only occurred at a later stage in mosaic's development, it is probable that their size was originally due to technical limitations. A mosaicist crouches or kneels to lay a floor and the amount of work he can do at any one time is limited to his arm's reach. In the case of large floors, several artisans can work at the same time, each on his own section, but this too will be restricted. Only when detailed planning had evolved was it possible to have each craftsman working on his own section of a large, overall design. The oldest mosaic hitherto discovered, at Gordium in Asia Minor, which according to archaeologists dates from the eighth century B.C., gives a telltale impression of a number of separate pieces of work having been "patchworked" together, each artisan having created his own little piece according to the dictates of his imagination and culture.

Neither this mosaic nor the others discovered at Gordium (which have been dated to the sixth and fifth centuries B.C.) were tessellated mosaics: they were made with pebbles. This is an extremely ancient technique which survives to this day in pebble mosaics in the Greek islands and in gardens on the Ligurian coast of Italy. In the fourth century B.C., however, this minor art form underwent a radical transformation and reached impressively high levels of craftsmanship. This change is well attested by such masterpieces as the pavements discovered in 1955–63 at Pella in Macedonia, Alexander the Great's birthplace. From the beginning of the third century B.C. or the end of the previous century, mosaics gave proof of an intelligent and sensitive application to the modest craft of decorative pavements of the principles evolved by the great Hellenic painters. The pebbles were selected so as to ensure contrasting colours and, most importantly, to achieve subtle gradations of shade and light, making the figures stand out, with thin slivers of lead inserted into the mortar outlining the contours. Eleven subjects are portrayed, among them Dionysus riding the panther, a scene from the Amazonomachia and the Rape of Helen. Some scholars have identified the scene of the lion hunt as a reflection of the famous votive offering which Craterus made to the Gods when he had saved his friend Alexander's life during a perilous hunting expedition. Although scenes of Alexander and the Lion Hunt usually show the huntsmen on horseback, the Pella panel may well be a version of the famous picture only stressing a moment of great peril rather than simply portraying a group of grave and formal horsemen. Another mosaic shows a staghunt. The dog has sunk its teeth into the prey, one of the two huntsmen is just about to administer the fatal blow while the other, grasping its antlers, has had his hat blown away up to the penultimate letter of the artist's signature: *Gnosis epoiesen* (Gnosis fecit). And Gnosis had good reason to be proud of his work; he even had caulicoles of acanthus winding along the border of his mosaic forming a spiral ornament of the utmost delicacy, and used different shades of colour to achieve a brilliant effect of perspective. Other pebble mosaics have survived at Delos, Olynthus, Eretria, Sicyon, Rhodes and elsewhere. Although they are not as outstanding as the Pella mosaic, they all have equally rich borders framing subjects from the same series of myths familiar through our knowledge of vases and paintings of antiquity: Bellerophon, Dionysus, gryphons and Chimeras. A second phase is attested by a tendency to polish the surface, followed by the insertion of proper mosaic cubes between the pebbles. A mosaic which was discovered at Shatby in Alexandria, Egypt, and which has been preserved in situ, has an elaborate border with various animals framing a scene of three hunters closing in on a stag. Both the border and the panel are composed of large, square multicoloured tesserae, but pebbles have been used for the mane of a lion, the tuft of hair on a bull's head and the hunters' hair, and for some small flowers and other ornamentation. Here we have a mixed technique but it does not necessarily mean that this was a transitional phase. Strips of lead have been extensively used for outlining detail, just as they were in pebble mosaics. In W. A. Daszewski's most recent articles, he dates the Shatby mosaic as later than the one in Pella but still from the third century B.C., and thus an earlier example than other pebble mosaics discovered in Sicily at Morgantina (Serra Orlando), which date from 260–250 B.C.

Pliny was in no doubt that mosaic was a Hellenic invention: "*pavimenta originem apud Graecos habent*"; and was aware that Pergamum must have been an important mosaic center. He thought particularly highly of the Greek, Sosos (the only mosaicist he mentions by name) for having invented the type of mosaic pavement known as *asaroton oecon* (an unswept room). Sosos used small, artificially coloured tesserae to achieve his colour effects: "*fecerat parvis e tessellis tinctisque in varios colores.*" This master craftsman of the second century B.C. was particularly famous for having created a picture of doves perched on the edge of a vase. Roman copies of this composition have survived, and at least one of them bears the artist's signature in Greek. An unpretentious version of the doves and vase theme with the artist's name in Greek is now in Rome's Capitoline Museum. The Romans were very fond of having copies made of the *asaroton*, the white unswept floor strewn with the remains of a feast. The oldest extant example dates from the pre-imperial era and is a pavement from a house in Aquileia; the latest a Roman pavement discovered in the Aventine area of Rome and now in the Vatican Museums.

When Pompeii was excavated, small-scale mosaics were found; the *emblemata*, which were made in workshops and then inserted into the floor of a room. As in the Sosos mosaic, in two other famous Pompeii mosaics with scenes from Greek theater, the signature of *Dioskourides Samios*, Dioskurides of Samos, could well have been that of the workman and not of the artist.

The *emblema* enjoyed lasting popularity in the Greek world. Sometimes these were genuine mosaics, reproductions of a famous work of art which were completed elsewhere and then placed within a wide border on site. Their popularity was in part due to the relatively small size of the rooms for which they were designed and the arrangement of the *klynai*, the couches on which the assembled company reclined to eat. These *klynai* were arranged on three sides of the room, leaving a free space in its center open to the gaze of the recumbent diners.

The floor in the first room of the House of the Drinking Contest of Antioch, dating from the third century A.D., has a very simple frame which was probably completely hidden by the couches. Next (working towards the center) comes a wide border in the shape of the Greek letter *p* (pi) containing a variety of geometrical shapes and enclosing the scene from which the house takes its name: the competition between Heracles and Dionysus as to who could drink the most. The scene is framed by a sumptuous, theatrical surround making use of perspective which is not only effective when standing in the center of the mosaic but also from any one of its four sides. Through the use of perspective, foreshortening and other three-dimensional devices, the geometric detail which borders the picture seems first to suggest depth, then stand out in relief in response to each viewer's varying visual response.

Emblemata were carried out in *opus vermiculatum*, marble or stone broken into tiny fragments and shaped irregularly, then arranged in rows which, rather like the incision of an engraving tool, traced out the pattern. This added more emphasis to the forms of the figures than just colour, light and shade would. The technique differed from that of *opus tessellatum*, in which the tesserae were all cubes of the same size. Sometimes the main decorative details and figures were worked in *vermiculatum* with the background and border in *tessellatum*. Such a degree of technical complexity meant that patterns had to be available, with highly experienced master craftsmen working in teams. Two *emblemata* which differ greatly in style but are both versions of the same picture, an official portrait of Queen Berenice II (246–222 B.C.), were found at Thmuis (Tell Timai) in Egypt. One is signed Sophilos and both must date from around 200 B.C. This indicates that at this time Alexandria, as well as Pergamum, was an important center for the design and production of *emblemata*. The mosaic by Sophilos is, in fact, one of the earliest in *opus vermiculatum* known to exist. If its dating at around 200 B.C. proves correct, it pre-dates even Hephaestion's mosaic. Alexandria was not only the center of a region where mosaicists practiced their art, it provided a pool of skilled craftsmen who travelled far and wide. An *emblema* in the House of the Faun in Pompeii depicts a satyr coupling with a nymph, almost identical to a mosaic made in Tell Timai. Together with other similarities which link Pompeii's mosaics with those of Egypt, this builds up evidence which enables us to trace the establishment of specialized production originating in the region of Alexandria. Again, the House of the Faun provides us with a mosaic, most probably of Alexandrine origin, showing a cat that has caught a partridge and this house originally contained what is probably the most famous ancient mosaic, the *Alexander and Darius at the Battle of Isus*, now in the National Archaeological Museum of Naples.

Pliny supplies us with yet another piece of valuable information: in Italy, pavements inlaid with stones (*lithostrata*) started at the time of the Emperor Sulla and were made with small slabs (*parvolis certe crustis*). He tells us that an example had survived in the Temple of Fortuna at Palestrina (Praeneste). Since the temple at Palestrina contains one of the most fascinating mosaics of antiquity, it was tempting to conclude that they were one and the same, only that the technical term *crustae* must mean carved slabs of marble and not the tiny tesserae of the Palestrina mosaic. An exhaustive study by G. Gullini of this mosaic, which represents an immense view of the Nile valley teeming with men and animals, has established its links with Alexandrine originals which could have been widely available through books of designs. Those responsible for this enchanting mosaic certainly knew Greek and were familiar with the animals they depicted, even mythical ones, such as the sphinx or a strange mixture of species which appears to include a baboon. Not only are the names of the animals written correctly in Greek but, as Margherita Guarducci has pointed out, these master artists were familiar with the legend of lapis lazuli being the open eyes of mountains, where they were found to occur naturally. Many lapis lazuli stones have been incorporated in the mosaic, adding yet another intriguing detail to this fascinating scene.

A Hellenic mosaic in black and white pebbles can still be seen on the Island of Mozia opposite the port of Marsala (western Sicily) in a stretch of water known as the Stagnone. By using only two colours, the work could be completed more quickly and materials were more likely to be found close to the site. This meant that two-colour mosaics were the ideal practical solution to the vast amount of work entailed in covering the enormous areas of Roman public buildings such as baths, basilicas and large market places. From the start this choice was accompanied by an analysis of the complex language of Hellenic painting in order to find simplified yet no less lively, adaptable and elegant versions in mosaic. This obviously involved doing away with the fragile distinction between *vermiculatum* and *tessellatum* as the craftsmen's job was now to construct a seamless covering for a large surface area. A stock of geometrical and floral decorations had to be created which could be converted into patterns and sections and inserted as work progressed while following very precise measurements. The planning process therefore assumed the utmost importance for the successful completion of projects. The laying of mosaics now involved much more repetitive work and could therefore be entrusted to less skilled workmen. Mosaic became architecture. It could be imbued with the grandiosity of public baths or assume a humble but cheerful character on the thresholds of the shops in Pompeii or Ostia, under the colonnades of the maritime guilds of Ostia or in the markets of other important ports such as Rimini. It could display a revealing picture of life within the confined space of a tomb or, quite simply, a warning to the unwary that there was a fierce dog on guard. This led to great changes in the style of mosaic. The images were now nearly always black on a white background as in the magnificent procession of sea life (*thiasos*) in the Baths of Neptune at Ostia, with its tritons, Nereids, sea lions and sea horses. The curves of the creatures' bodies are picked out with outlines of white tesserae, in a concise and vigorous language, spelling an end to the modulation of Hellenic plasticity. This shift to more disparate, autonomous images is noticeable when comparing these mosaics from the Baths of Neptune with others at Ostia which were inspired by them, such as those in the Baths of Buticosus. Becatti attributes these to the same mosaicist who depicts the living forms in all sorts of attitudes: v-shapes, zig-zags and spirals.

On occasion the blatantly ornamental quality of the work leads to an inversion of colour, in an alternation of negative and positive. White figures advance across a black background or, as in the wonderful mosaic in the palestra of the Caracalla baths, a frieze of white dolphins is set on a black field surrounding a maritime scene in black on white. This type of mosaic has never been envisaged as anything else but a floor decoration. There is no intention of reproducing a great work of art, for which its limited technique is ill-suited. The patterns are sometimes derivative but always suited to their context of pavement decoration. Black and white mosaic is the result of a long developmental process in Italian decorative art, beginning with the adoption of a mortar of crushed potsherds to cover pavements and evolving towards *opus signinum*, fragments of coloured marble laid at random in a mortar of volcanic sand, *pozzolana*, mixed with lime and broken terracotta tiles. During the first century A.D. mosaicists who had learnt their craft in Rome used to scatter fragments of coloured marble in the background of black or white tesserae. Examples are to be found in tessellated pavements in Rome itself, to the south of Rome and also, but less frequently, in Aquileia and Pola.

Apart from picture mosaics, this technique was also well suited to the exploitation of decorative motifs which were versatile and yet based on a rigorous though uncomplicated geometry. The regularity of the motifs is reminiscent of textile designs and this was perhaps the inspiration for the fringing which sometimes surrounds the central field, like a carpet. Roman mosaicists turned the scalloped edges into an architectural reference, making them battlements or towers, emphasizing the function of the border which enclosed the central design like a boundary. Another innovation was to reorganize the available space by turning the border into a setting where fantasies could be indulged in the form of dolphins with leafy tails, heads made out of acanthus leaves and vines full of birds.

The Italic roots of black and white mosaics are clear from their rarity outside the peninsula and, more particularly, outside central Italy. In one of the few examples ever discovered in the East, the details of the figures are painted in rather than being depicted with tesserae. Black and white mosaics did not, of course, supplant coloured ones. Some fine examples of the latter date from the time of the Emperor Hadrian, but their ornamentation is more austere. Images of plant life have disappeared, their place taken by meanders exploiting perspective and other architectonic themes. Mosaics of this era were being used to embellish the vaults in the great and original monuments of Hadrian's era. The era of Hadrian and the Antonine emperors marked the high point of the Roman art of black and white mosaics. From the third century onwards, mosaics which used several colours, in Rome and elsewhere, are the most worthy of study, but the marriage of mosaic and architecture achieved by the black and white technique certainly lent drama to wall mosaics. The famous portraits of athletes in the Baths of Caracalla are a good example, and probably date from the end of the third century or the beginning of the fourth.

The varying fortunes of mosaic north of the Alps were linked to political events. In Gaul the first pavement mosaics were begun around 50 A.D. and the art died out at the time of the Germanic invasions of 260–275 A.D. In Pannonia the defeat of the Romans at Adrianople in 378 A.D. put an end to all such artistic activity. Mosaic turns out to be a very useful yardstick by which to measure the resilience of societies which knew they were under threat. The large number of mosaics which survive from Gaul show a preponderance of geometric motifs taken from Italic black and white mosaics, but with far greater density, sometimes appearing in a thick mesh of rectangles and squares; others have *emblemata* joined by a network of chains which meet to form swastikas (Musée Guimet, Paris and Musée Saint-Pierre, Lyons). Some of the *emblemata* are naive and simple versions of famous scenes, such as *The drunken Dionysus watched by all the gods of Olympus*, a mosaic from Vienne which is now at the Musée Saint-Pierre in Lyons. Marine scenes are rarer, although one example in the border of a very lively and imaginative mosaic from Lyons has survived, its central section divided into a complex geometric design with decorative motifs. Hadrian's Wall bought time for Roman Britain and over six hundred mosaics have been discovered most of which date from 300 to 370 A.D. The very earliest mosaics in Britain are from 60–70 A.D. (in the legionary fortress baths in Exeter, Isca Dumnoniorum) and were by Italic mosaicists. Later on, indigenous craftsmen learned the art and proved very conservative in their approach to technique (an *opus signinum* pavement in London dates from 130 A.D. whereas none of this type had been constructed in Italy since pre-imperial times). They were also faithful to the Roman themes, as the exceptional pavement at Lullingstone proves: halfway through the fourth century we have the tragic love of Dido for Aeneas played out in several scenes. Again at Lullingstone there is a mosaic of Europa and the Bull, while Orpheus, Ceres, Triptolemus, Lycurgus and Ambrosia, Perseus and Andromeda and other heroes people the mosaics at Brading. It is tempting to wonder whether these are merely the literary references of a community which has remained faithful to the traditions of Latium, even so far removed from the cultural homeland, or whether they betray a resistance to the spread of the Christian religion.

In the Iberian peninsula the story was completely different. Mosaics date from as early as the seventh century B.C., in the form of pebble pavements discovered in tombs at Muela de Castulo (Jaén) which show similarities in technique with those of Gordium. No discovery has yet been made to bridge the gap between these very old mosaics and those of the Roman era up to the sixth century. However, the aspirations of the Iberian mosaicists and their Mediterranean links are recorded by the large mosaic from the triclinium of the House of Mitreus in Mérida. This work has been identified as a reproduction of a famous painting of late antiquity, the *Cosmology*, which Procopius of Gaza described in such depth, pointing out all its mythological references.

While mosaicists in Gaul adapted the geometric patterns of Roman black and white mosaics to their own coloured versions, the Iberians were exposed to many different influences and displayed remarkable technical skill, especially in the plentiful use of artificial colours such as green and blue, suggesting an expertise which is confirmed by the presence of "signed" mosaics (one, in Mérida, is signed *ex officina Anniponi* [from the workshop of Anniponus]). The existence of landed estates, with their effective private armies, meant that the privileged and most Romanized classes preserved their internal social structure when the Vandals invaded and when the Kingdom of the Goths was established. Thus in the peninsula's large country villas and sometimes in the cities as well, mosaic ran its full developmental course.

All over the world in late classical times *emblemata* were made and inserted into a wider geometrical design which took up the whole of the pavement and the Iberian peninsula was no exception. Scenes depicted included the games held in the Roman circuses, hunts and episodes from the Trojan Cycle as in the remarkably fine mosaic of Achilles in Skyros at Pedrosa de la Vega. In this scene from Greek heroic literature, Rea, wife of Lycomedes, is seen standing behind the curtain of the gynaeceum at a little distance from her maidservant, reminiscent of Theodora's handmaiden in the mosaic of the Empress and her suite in Ravenna. Many of the *tesserae* of the white background are regularly placed, following the arrangement of palmettes or cones. This design is found in other mosaics of the late classical period in Iberia (the Pedrosa pavement dates from around the end of the fourth century) and was to be exploited to its fullest effect in the Great Palace of Constantinople.

The mosaics found at Santisteban del Puerto are probably of later date, for despite their classical subjects (from the stories of Achilles) and the late classical inscriptions, they are full of exaggerated linear detail and bold flourishes, giving them a medieval flavour. In contrast to Santisteban's isolation on the periphery of Europe with its calm and creativity, Egara (Tarrasa), to the north of Barcelona, tells us a great deal about the period from the middle of the fourth century to the eleventh century. In Catalonia we can see how the tradition developed of combining tessellated pavements with the newer wall mosaic coverings for vaults. In the Constantinian mausoleum at Centcelles the interior of the dome is decorated with several horizontal panels, the longest of which at the bottom shows a hunting scene, borrowing a theme typical of pavement mosaics.

The highly original Iberian mosaics were inspired by the new life breathed into the art in flourishing North African centers. The widespread use of black and white mosaic in Rome and in central Italy was contemporaneous with work in coloured mosaic which was very traditional in character and perpetuated the Hellenic style. In Africa and in the East, where colour had never been forsaken, mosaic fulfilled many roles: it created a suitable setting in sumptuous buildings, the *emblemata* being positioned to greatest effect, as if laying a "permanent carpet" (in the so-called "House with a Table laid for a Banquet" at Antioch, Doro Levi and Jean Lassus have rightly identified the function of one *emblema* as that of a magnificent bedside-rug). Mosaics also indicated the uses to which a room was put: the designs would be carefully chosen and the size of the motifs varied according to the proportions of the room. The area covered by the scene was gradually enlarged until it occupied almost the whole surface of the floor, sometimes echoing the divisions of the vault and making the room a harmonious whole. The repetition of many small motifs, like a piece of patterned cloth or a carpet, furnished both small and large rooms. As the role of mosaic became more all-embracing, the imitative perfection of the *emblemata* was discarded and different techniques merged; the distinction between *vermiculatum* and *tessellatum* was abandoned. Figures were simplified and sometimes enlarged, with white backgrounds being favoured to enhance the effect of rich colours; the rigid geometrical sections were thought to contribute little and *trompe l'oeil* versions were substituted, or underwent a metamorphosis into very realistic and luxuriant images of plant life.

The North African master artists endowed similar decorative details with a tremendous baroque exuberance, creating festoons of acanthus which spread all over a pavement at Timgad, almost reducing the *emblema* which they enclosed to a miniature. At Sabratha the second-century Christian mosaic busts prefigure the sixth century's work in Ravenna. There are gory and dramatic scenes of prisoners who have been condemned *ad bestias* (to be killed by wild animals) in Zlitan, Libya. Geographical panoramas recur, sometimes as naturalistic landscapes, others like pieces in a child's game (Tabarka, Carthage); there are stirring hunting scenes (Bone); everyday scenes of fishing (Sousse); harvesting grapes (Cherchel) while others repeat scenes from epic poems (*Achilles in Skyros* (Sousse)): the breadth of subject matter shows what creative freedom these North African mosaicists enjoyed. The Byzantine reconquest meant that many churches were restored in these regions; other buildings also benefited. According to a recent theory, the famous *Lady of Carthage* depicts the Empress Theodora.

The North African mosaicists did not only leave their mark in the Iberian peninsula. Signs of their influence are to be found in Italy and, with particular frequency, in Sicily. Even a cursory examination reveals distinct schools of mosaic, with notable stylistic resemblances between the work at the villa of Piazza Armerina and that found at Thuburbo Majus, El-Dje and Henchir-el-Kasbat in Africa. Piazza Armerina is not an isolated case: another large villa with mosaics from the same school has now been discovered to the south of Syracuse, near Eloro (Villa del Tellaro).

The other center of mosaic in late antiquity is Syria, where the tessellated pavements of Antioch (first revealed to the world at large when Doro Levi published his exhaustive work on them) provide plenty of examples, together with a number of other mosaics found in villages, towns and provincial capitals. The influence of the Syrian "baroque" school even found its way to the Euphrates Valley but other influences were also at work, of Eastern origin, which were to lead to the complete destruction of Hellenic naturalism. Extreme examples of the swing away from the classical world's style are found in Edessa's second- and third-century mosaics, with their full-length frontal portraits of people in Eastern costume. Only a few decorative details of the border (a chain motif) remain to remind us that mosaic had originated and developed in a Mediterranean culture. Mosaic was not only sought after around the Mediterranean basin and along those Atlantic shores where the Roman Empire held sway. Far away in Armenia, in a building which has been identified as the palace of Tiridates the Great, ruler of Armenia, a hypocaust (the system of underfloor central heating invented by the Romans) and baths have been discovered. The room has a mosaic pavement, of Greek craftsmanship dating from the third century A.D. with a border of dolphins, hunters and gods of the sea. In the center are busts of Okeanos and Thalassios with a surprising inscription: *meden labontes ergasametha* (we take nothing for our work), a tribute to the generosity of the gods of the sea, revealing an ethos very different from that of the mercantile society in which mosaic had flourished.

On page 17: Pella, Macedonia. Detail from the *Lion Hunt* mosaic in pebbles, outlines in lead strips, 375–300 B.C.

Left: detail of an *asaroton* (unswept floor) from a villa on the Aventine, second century A.D., Vatican Museum, Rome. The *asaroton* motif was created by Sosos of Pergamum, second century A.D.

Below: *Cat catching a partridge and marine still life*, from the House of the Faun at Pompeii, now in the National Archaeological Museum, Naples. Late first century A.D. The cat and bird motif stems from Alexandrian models.

Opposite: *Comedy scene with musicians. Emblema* from a room in Cicero's house at Pompeii, signed by Dioskurides of Samos, c. 100 B.C. A perfect version of a third-century B.C. painting. National Archaeological Museum, Naples.

Below and opposite: Palestrina (Praeneste), mosaic in Palazzo Barberini, part of the Temple of Fortuna. The large composition with Nilotic landscape was probably carried out by Alexandrian craftsmen on first-century B.C. Alexandrian models. The pictures of exotic or fantastic animals and of lapis lazuli as blue eyes in rocks point to an Alexandrian origin. The removal of the mosaic from the sanctuary to the palace led to considerable restoration, visible in the center of the detail from the same mosaic reproduced opposite, which depicts an *Offering before the temple*.

On pages 24–25: *Alexander and Darius at the Battle of Isus*, from the House of the Faun at Pompeii. Between 200 and 100 B.C. National Archaeological Museum, Naples. The large mosaic (342 × 592 cm [11 × 19 ft]), set directly into the floor with local stone and a few glass tesserae, probably reproduces the painting by Philoxenus of Eretria, famous for inventing four-colour painting (fourth century B.C.).

Opposite and below: Pompeii,
nymphaeum in the garden of the House
of the Scientists. Mosaics in stone and
glass tesserae with borders of seashells.
First century B.C.

Below: fragment of floor in black and white tesserae, with putti on sea monsters. Third century A.D. Baths of Caracalla, Rome.

Opposite: *Rape of Europa*, floor mosaic from the bedroom of a Roman villa at Aquileia. Late first century A.D. Archaeological Museum, Aquileia.

Below: *Scene of port life*. Discovered in 1975 in the historical center of Rimini, this mosaic in black and white tesserae (second century A.D.) shows a merchant vessel entering port preceded by a pinnace. From the triclinium of a house probably owned by a merchant or chandler. Civic Museum, Rimini.

Opposite: *Bust of an athlete*, in part of a mosaic floor found in a room next to the north gymnasium of Aquileia (first century A.D.). Museum of Archaeology, Aquileia.

Below: this mosaic, personifying *Soteria* (Hope) was originally at the center of an eight-pointed star in the cold-room of the Baths of Apolausis at Antioch. It is an example of the sophistication of fourth-century A.D. mosaic art in Antioch. Mosaic Museum, Antioch.

Below: *Orpheus* playing to animals. Panel from Tarsus. Mosaic Museum, Antakya. With two other panels in a rich and varied decoration, this is a fine example of the almost "Baroque" Antioch mosaics of the third century A.D.

Opposite: the world of actors, dear to Greek vase painters, is a favourite with Syrian mosaicists. The author of this *emblema* from Antioch (second century A.D., now at Princeton University) draws on the theater to make his images recognizable and immediate. The scene shows the moment when Iphigenia is called by Clytemnestra to disquiet Agamemnon. A coin of Marcus Aurelius found under the floor establishes the date of this mosaic.

On page 36 above: Sousse, on the east coast of Tunisia, stands on the site of ancient Hadrumetum, a Phoenician and subsequently Roman colony reformed by Trajan. From the villas round the town come many great mosaics largely preserved in the local museum, such as this second-century A.D. *Sea Scene* (detail shown).

On page 36 below: a subject dear to the vast African mosaics, to reappear in the peristyle pavement of the great Imperial Palace of Constantinople, is the hunt. In this detail from a large composition (third to fourth century A.D.) the two lions rending a boar show the rare painterly skills of African mosaic.

On page 37: *The Four Seasons* (third century A.D.). Archaeological Museum, Tripoli. The panels in mosaic alternate with ones in African marble.

Opposite above: *Two female centaurs crowning Venus*. Floor mosaic from the Villa of Elles, near Le Kef (late third or early fourth century A.D.). Bardo Museum, Tunis. The inscription "*Polystefanus rationis est Archeus*" remains enigmatic.

Opposite below: *Country house in vineyard*, Bardo Museum, Tunis. In a room with three half domes in a house near Tabarka unearthed in 1890, three mosaics were found (all now in Tunis), picturing three aspects of a prosperous farming estate of the fourth century A.D.

Below: floor with *Zodiac Signs* within a complex geometric design, probably to match the panelling of the vault (second century A.D.). Bardo Museum, Tunis.

Left: part of a large mosaic discovered in 1779 at the ancient site of Lorium on the Via Aurelia, a few miles outside Rome. It must have been an octagon containing twenty-four hexagons, about 1 m (3 ft) across, and three trapeziums connected by spiral motifs. All depict theatrical subjects, like the one reproduced here. The work dates from the third century A.D. Vatican Museums.

Right: part of the large *Dionysian Mosaic* found in Cologne (third century A.D.). Archaeological Museum, Cologne.

Below: Lullingstone, Kent. Floor of the
Roman Villa with scenes from the *Aeneid*
and, at the center, Venus between two
cupids with torches. Fourth century A.D.

Below: Hunting Scene from the peristyle of a village at Tusculum, Rome (end of third century A.D.). Galleria Borghese, Rome.

On page 44: mosaic floor found in Faenza in 1971–2, showing a central scene bordered by a geometric cornice panel. In terms of archaeological features dated fifth century, perhaps showing the Emperor Honorius with bodyguards and general Stilicho. Alternatively, it could represent Ulysses finding Achilles giving him arms, which would be further evidence of the interest in classical culture in declining Roman society. Civic Museum, Faenza.

THE CHRISTIAN WORLD

Our knowledge of ancient wall mosaics is somewhat limited. Traces can be found in a few more minor monuments, such as a niche from a rural pagan sanctuary (now in the Vatican Museums) with an image of the god Silvanus with his axe. The mosaic consists of glass tesserae and the luster of the whole results partly from arranging them at different angles to the background, partly from greater spacing. Dating from the third century A.D., it is a forerunner of Christian mosaics. In the necropolis underneath St Peter's in the Vatican a small mausoleum was discovered from the period just before Constantine when Christianity and the Sun cult were being fused. A mosaic decoration covered the walls and the small vault, depicting Christ in the chariot of the sun god with rays emanating from his head and a vine spread over the yellow background. The wall mosaics have fallen but their bed remains visible and reveals traces of Christian themes.

The Mausoleum of Santa Costanza was built in Rome about 360 A.D. for Constantine's daughter. The cupola was destroyed in the seventeenth century but the design is preserved in old drawings. Two thirds of the mosaic showed Old Testament scenes below and New Testament ones above; candelabrum-like acanthus scrolls interspersed with panthers and caryatids divided the dome into sectors. The unifying feature of the mosaic was a Nilotic landscape along the whole base. As a whole it shows that, even fifty years after Constantine's edict extending rights and toleration to Christians, no independent Christian imagery existed. The barrel vaults of the walkway round the central space with cupola are decorated with large panels in which various ornamental motifs are repeated. One is purely geometrical, another has a pattern incorporating various human and animal figures, amongst which there are miniature pictures of Psyche, a Neoplatonic, non-Christian symbol. Other panels show vintage scenes, with putti climbing through the foliage or conveying bunches of grapes on ox-drawn carts to the presses in the charge of further putti. The Dionysiac theme of these scenes could be reinterpreted in Christian terms, stressing the Eucharistic role of wine. The most remarkable panels exalt wine in their depicture of the silver plate used for funeral libations. The objects are enlivened with splashes of gold; glass is amply used, but natural stone prevails.

Santa Costanza has yet a third decorated area, namely the niches. In two of them, both semicircular, there are ancient mosaics which have been partly restored. The subjects, probably copied from large-scale designs in church apses, show two variants of Christ carrying the Law; in one, He stands on a rock and hands the scroll to Peter, while in the better preserved one He sits on a sphere. Both the head and body of Christ are probably original, except for minor restorations and provide valuable insight into early fourth-century style. The colour and painterly touch of the design seems at odds with the rather late dating, which is, however, soundly based. In this style, colour is still vital in creating form, and, as the purple pallium shows, an optical effect is realized through uniting colours. The purple is achieved by means of tesserae with strongly contrasting colours, such as dark red, green and light blue tending towards grey, which in our perception merge like the multicoloured brush strokes of the pointillists. At that stage, wall mosaics had become quite mature and had developed subtle methods for creating images to be viewed and admired from a certain distance.

As this example shows, mosaics may be studied in several ways, of which two have long traditions: iconography based on the themes shown, and style. Of equal weight is the more recent study of technique details as a tool for probing and clarifying the aims of artist and client. It is difficult to trace the development of wall mosaic during the first centuries of Christianity with any degree of continuity. So much has been destroyed that only fragments of the total production survive. Floor mosaics of this period are more common, since whole pavements or fragments seem to appear wherever archaeologists excavate. True masterpieces have been unearthed in cities of late antiquity throughout the Roman Empire, from Britain to North Africa, from Spain to

Mesopotamia. North African craftsmen were masters in mosaic art and helped to spread the new style of the third century in which mosaics were no longer divided into panels and pavements were designed as large scenes over the whole surface. Amongst the most spectacular are the well preserved large pavements of the villa of Piazza Armerina in Sicily, the date of which remains controversial; a part at least is from the early fourth century. The mosaic of the *Great Hunt*, with the famous portrait of the villa's majestic owner in the garb of grand master of the hunt, is probably the best known of those unearthed at the villa, but the finest example of style is found in the villa's triclinium with three apses, where the labours of Hercules are shown in unmitigated, primitive brutality. The scattered tesserae, some in glass, found in the soil that covered the mosaic show that the vaults too were faced with them.

In Christian churches, the figurative function of floor mosaics gradually diminished. However, there is one early Christian pavement with symbolic figures that play a vital role to be found in the two basilicas, dated to just before Constantine, under the cathedral of Aquileia. Amongst the many themes we have Jonah being cast as food to the whale. In one panel, the Eucharist in the form of a basket of bread, is crowned by a Victory. The apse of Santa Pudenziana in Rome, a bath transformed into a church (rebuilt and decorated about 390), contains the oldest extant mosaic in a Christian church. Christ is enthroned amongst the apostles in an open porch that reproduces an actual structure, namely the monumental courtyard that enclosed Golgotha in Jerusalem. Thus Christ was located in a sacred Mediterranean place known to many, which made the picture real and convincing.

The method for realizing wall mosaics was of course derived from that for pavements, but with refinements. To prepare the surface, at least three layers of successively finer mortar were applied (for pavements, often only two layers); cubic tesserae were stuck to the last layer, which contained powdered marble, giving cohesion and bright whiteness. This layer hardened quickly, and was spread only over an area that could be covered with tesserae in one day's work. Before inserting the pieces, the artist would sketch the design on the moist mortar, and mark the main colour areas with wide light brush strokes; for example, the parts to take gold-coloured tesserae were coloured yellow or bright red. Tesserae were mostly of coloured glass in all hues. Large cakes of glass were carried from the workshops to the work place, where they were cut into fairly regular small cubes (about 1 cm [½ in] square). These were used for most of the compositions, but for finer details like heads or folds in clothing, irregularly cut pieces of varying size were needed to cope with the design and the artist had a variety of cakes on the scaffold where he worked. Gold tesserae were cut from similar cakes, made of translucent stained glass covered with gold-leaf and immersed in protective glass powder that hardened on further firing in a kiln. All glassy material of that period was lustrous and very refractive; however, in early medieval times, especially in the Eastern Empire, too uniform and brilliant effects tended to be shunned: less shining or even opaque glass was used to modulate mosaic surfaces.

We do not know how many mosaicists worked in Italy as a whole, nor whether in areas where many fourth-century churches were built artists were locals or itinerant teams from a few important centers. Presumably every large town had a number of its own workshops to meet local demand. One square meter of mosaic has about ten thousand tesserae all placed by hand (the thumb is the artist's main tool) and the attendant technology, particularly the supply of large quantities of glass, presupposed fairly large and complex organization. In one of the late fourth-century small mosaics in the chapel of St Aquilinus in San Lorenzo Maggiore, Milan, we observe the hands of at least three or four different artists. The chapel, originally a mausoleum and probably imperial, belongs to the period of the great St Ambrose when Milan was at its most influential as the capital of the Western Empire. In the scene of Christ dressed as a young philosopher speaking to the apostles, elements almost obsolete at the time are joined with others that are radically new. Amongst the latter is the gold ground, here appearing for the first time. That several artists were involved is apparent in vital parts of the work, such as the shape of the heads. Some apostles have soft features and fragile outlines that might be called conservative, others show a stronger play of light and shade, while a third group are in more violent and saturated colours.

Another later small chapel in Milan exemplifies developments in Milanese mosaic style: the chapel of San Vittore in Cielo d'Oro (St Victor in golden heaven) whose very name suggests the fascination it exerted. It is a kind of golden reliquary, a shrine with a gold cover, now within the larger church of Sant'Ambrogio. The bust of St Victor, set in a medallion, stands out from a shining gold ground; on the walls, figures of other saints are surrounded by intense blue like that of the third-century mosaic of Silvanus mentioned earlier. The vaults are mainly in a simpler style with garments stiffer than those in the chapel of St Aquilinus. Naples, another great Christian city, must have had churches adorned with large mosaics, almost wholly lost today. But for the mosaics in the baptistry of the Cathedral of San Giovanni in Fonte (early fifth century), we should be unaware of what must have been the Neapolitan school of mosaic. Many mosaics in the baptistry have fallen, but some parts remain intact. Not all vestiges of pagan symbolism have disappeared, though the most glaring ones have been removed.

Santa Maria Maggiore in Rome, a basilica built and decorated under Sixtus III (432–440), is the only fifth-century example extant. It was one of Rome's largest basilicas and the first built independently by the bishop. The apse was destroyed in the thirteenth century when the church was enlarged, but the triumphal arch and nave retain their fifth-century mosaics. The stories of Christ's infancy on the arch are treated in an unusual way, raising absorbing questions: the angels are gathered in groups like guards of the imperial palace; in the scene showing the adoration of the Magi, the infant Jesus is on a throne instead of on his mother's lap; in all scenes Mary wears gold-embroidered clothes like a court lady. Another unusual feature is the continuity of the scenes without break, as in a temple frieze or triumphal arch. The walls of the nave are an extension of this project, in richly unfolding Old Testament scenes that show the deeds of Christ's forerunners in panels (2 × 2 m [6½ × 6½ ft]) under each window.

The mosaics of Santa Maria Maggiore are a good example of what we might call "functional colouring" in early Christian mosaics. In big churches the images were quite far from the congregation so that powerful means were needed to put across visual messages which in time resulted in an almost explosive heightening of colour tone in the fifth century. The timid illusionism of the transition period used a style in which foreground contours were vital, partly removing the need for previous colour contrasts and gradually changing the conventional combinations. Later came the use of a gold ground. In Santa Maria Maggiore we have a first step towards this phase. To begin with, only a gold strip was used, not a complete background. This introduces into the biblical stories, on panels in the nave and on friezes of the arch, a zone of strong but rather masked light, so that the more abstract features of the landscape merge. Lines of glass tesserae of dark greenish yellow, shining almost like gold, create barely discernible colour transitions between the lines and the clearer green tones of the landscape features. Simulating gold sheen by means of a special mix of stained glasses and softening the contrast with opaquer varieties of glass was a great artistic invention.

Ravenna inherited the artistic culture of Milan and became the next capital of the Western Empire. In the Mausoleum of Galla Placidia (440–450), built on a cruciform plan, there is a continuous flow of mosaic panels in the lunettes and large mosaics in the barrel vaults and cupola. The architectonic parts were now marked not by sculptured friezes but by ornamental strips within the mosaic, as if these identified strict rules for the arrangement of decorative elements. Non-figurative ornaments or symbols are sited on the curved surfaces of cupola and vaults, while on the vertical walls there are mainly figures and scenes, such as the Good Shepherd in the lunette above the entrance, and St Lawrence in the far lunette, while in the lunette under the dome we see the apostles standing in adoration of the Cross at the cupola's center or, as H. P. L'Orange has suggested, of Light as a symbol of the Lord.

In the Baptistry of the Orthodox, built about 450, large figures predominate. Mosaics separate the cupola into three bands, the lowest being richly adorned with columns flanking altars and thrones alternately. Then there is a series of large figures of apostles following Peter and Paul holding golden crosses and above, in the center of the cupola, a circular panel represents baptism, with the baptismal font found directly underneath. As O. Demus points out, there are principles of composition here that led Byzantine art to large, unified decoration where architecture forms an important constitutive element: the apostles are so arranged as to surround the baptismal scene, at which many of them seem to gaze, thus giving three-dimensional coherence to the two belts. With the illusion of depth and shape, the lower, architectural belt contributes to the impression of space in the cupola's mosaic decoration. Similar principles governed the one-time decoration in the huge cupola of the Church of St George at Salonika, whose date (about 400) suggests that these new forms came from the East.

In Sant'Apollinare Nuovo, one of the main structures built under the Ostrogoth king Theodoric after 496, we note how the decoration of basilicas evolved. In Santa Maria Maggiore, the nave was decorated by separate panels; here, in a sixth-century basilica, it covers every inch of the nave, whose walls are partitioned into three bands. The lowest originally showed Theodoric on the right wall and his queen on the left, at the head of a procession moving towards pictures of Christ and the Virgin enthroned, beside the bapistry; the procession and its royal members were erased when the Byzantines reconquered the city, and replaced by the extant train of saints. Above, between the windows, stands a group of Old Testament prophets, and the third band has a sequence of small panels with New Testament scenes, on the right the passion of Christ, on the left the miracles and parables. Large biblical pictures were a novelty, but perhaps followed new notions of using images imported from the East. The use of silver tesserae, more lustrous than golden ones, is much in evidence in the monuments of Salonika and in the oldest mosaics of Hagia Sophia in Istanbul. In the Christ scenes of Sant'Apollinare, He has a silver halo, as do the prophets standing in the window band. Further, the use of natural stone in quite delicate shades to render the flesh of faces, hands and bare parts of the body, is found in several sixth-century Ravenna mosaics, with forerunners found in the East. Craftsmen brought with them a special skill for cutting tesserae and assembling them in designs which achieved a unique sense of life in the portrayal of faces, balanced between an abstraction and a sketch.

Sant'Apollinare in Classe was consecrated by Bishop Maximianus in 547. The mosaics of the arch are the result of ancient and repeated restorations, but the arresting figures of angels with silver halos are sixth century, as are the mosaics in the apse, except for some restorations in the lower belts. In the apsidal conch, the saint is shown below with arms raised in prayer. At the top the transfiguration is shown symbolically: Christ, whose face is at the center of a cross set in a medallion, hovers between figures of Elijah and Moses, while below the apostles enter represented as sheep. The medallion stands out from a sky of pure gold, while the saint walks on a paradisiacal dark green ground rich in flowers, shrubs and birds. The composition probably results from two designs for the apse, which would explain its complexity.

Another building consecrated by Maximianus about 550 is San Vitale, a unique structure modelled on the cupola style of sixth-century Istanbul. The unknown architect developed the design into a cylinder girded by a lower one; from the center of the cupola the splendid choir projects upwards almost in Gothic style. It is a remarkable example of complex imagery, while affording a splendid view of a mosaic whole. The figurative elements are mainly in the apse and on the side walls, while the rest, from the lining of *opus sectile* (where the tesserae are cut to fit the contours of the design) in the lower part to the top of the choir vault, is covered with a set of ornaments and symbols cunningly blended with the colouring of the whole. Five large figures stand out in the apse, as had then become customary (another example is the apse of the Church SS. Cosma e Damiano in Rome, 526–530): Christ sitting on a sphere and clad in imperial purple, flanked by two angels similar to the guards found next to the imperial throne, and alongside these Bishop Ecclesius, founder of the church, in his role as donor and San Vitale, the saint to whom the church is dedicated. The side walls are adorned with Old Testament figures; at the center of one wall Abel and Melchisedek, symbols of the Eucharist, on the opposite wall Abraham and the three men who visited him at Mamre, a symbol of the same sacrament. At the top of the apse, flying angels carry a medallion with a cross, reminiscent of the goddess Victory; at the top of the vault reappear victory angels, four of them holding up a medallion containing the Lamb. They stand erect between the spirals of a fine green acanthus teeming with multicoloured exotic birds in the Roman manner, while the leaves have shades of strong blue and red, producing lively contrasts. On the lower walls of the apsidal niche are found the two panels already mentioned with Justinian and Theodora, probably inserted very late, when Ravenna had come under Byzantine rule again. Static figures almost depicted from in front, looking into infinity, the bodily shapes simplified and relieved only by the surface design of flattened folds – such is the "Justinian style" at its height, an ideological tool of the Byzantine ruler. The colour symbolism reaches its peak: the halo surrounding Justinian and his wife is marked by a single silver line, subtly alluding to their high position in the Christian hierarchy.

San Vitale has few traces of its original mosaic pavement divided into small panels as decorative strips. The panels show animals, birds and plant decorations in a simple style, modelled in large and strongly coloured tesserae, with a highly ornamental effect. The sixth century saw a revival of mosaic floors, in a simple style that needed no great expertise. From Christian art it passed to synagogues and finally recovered its ancient splendour in even finer form in the floors of villas of the Arab conquerors.

If Ravenna is a great chapter in the history of mosaic art, it is in Rome that we can follow its course with some continuity. Like the rest of Italy, Rome felt the Byzantine pressure and reacted as best it could, sometimes by submitting, other times by resisting and reaffirming its independence. These attitudes are reflected in the imagery chosen for mosaics. Thus, in the fifth century a picture was conceived in which the Lamb as symbol of the Lord is worshipped by His people: the enthroned Lamb receives homage from the twenty-four elders of the Apocalypse while the four mystic animals hover above. This scene was shown in huge mosaics, such as the choir arch in San Paolo-fuori-le-Mura commissioned by the princess Galla Placidia a little before 450. Probably in the eighth century, the basic symbol of the Lamb was replaced by the bust of Christ. Eastern theologians had no place for the Lamb, while in Rome it would have gained a political and religious meaning over time, most conspicuously expressed in the fifth century in the façade of St Peter's in the Vatican, in a mosaic reproduced in an eleventh-century miniature.

In the early sixth century, during the pontificate of Felix IV (526–530), a derelict building in the Forum of Vespasian was transformed into a church; it was dedicated to the performers of miracles, Saints Cosmas and Damian, and decorated with a large apsidal mosaic. The task was entrusted to a reputed workshop and so splendidly executed that one wonders how in a country struck by so many disasters the complex and costly art of a mosaic such as this could go on thriving. On the triumphal arch a picture of the Adoration of the Lamb unfolds, merging with the majestic decoration of the apse. Christ, in a scene of the second coming, clothed in a tunic and mantle of gold, descends over a background of intensely blue sky with a path of glowing clouds, while below on the green banks of the Jordan, Saints Peter and Paul with solemn gestures present the saints to whom the church is dedicated. At the sides we see the figures of the donor, Pope Felix, completely restored, and of Saint Theodore. At their feet, on a separate band, the Lamb appears on a mount from which spring the Rivers of Life. At each side, six sheep, symbols of the Apostles, advance in procession towards Christ. Like the composition on the arch, this band has a gold background. Another novelty, recently introduced into Italy, was the use of silver, seen here in the silver nimbus over the Lamb. The mosaic is made entirely of glass with no addition of natural stone, which may be due to strong local traditions.

In the mosaics of the triumphal arch in the Basilica of San Lorenzo-fuori-le-Mura, of the period of Pope Pelagius II (578–590), we see in the few heads untouched by later restoration what may have been the last work of the craftsmen that executed the mosaics for Felix IV. Some characteristic practices are still evident, such as the highly refined use of pink, reddish and greyish glass tesserae for faces. However, the drapes are flattened in this case.

Another problem in the development of mosaic is that information gathered from extant monuments of the early seventh century are often contradictory. There is a large collection of mosaics that must clearly be classified as coming under a prevailing Eastern influence. In the mosaics of Santo Stefano Rotondo and Sant'Agnese, which go back to Honorius I (625–638), mosaicists used Byzantine methods. This is seen especially in the apse of Sant'Agnese, where the three figures (St Agnes in imperial garb flanked by Popes Honorius and Symmachus, the latter in office around 500) are surrounded by a large expanse of gold. The mosaics in the Lateran Baptistry, of an only slightly later date, are in a different style. The oratory of St Venantius was decorated about 640. Here the technique based on glass tesserae once more prevails and is clearly adopted by genuine masters: the faces are modelled with fairly large tesserae and colours are strong.

Another important piece of mosaic art preserved in Rome, which is clearly Byzantine in style, is the series that John VII (705–707) had ordered for the chapel built in the old church of St Peter. When this was demolished in 1609, part of the mosaics were saved. The technique in these is openly derived from Constantinople with a superb rendering of flesh by means of small tesserae of natural stone, and many other sophisticated devices. The tesserae are deliberately quite far apart, which must have softened the shapes, almost to the point of the Hellenistic frescoes the same pope commissioned for Santa Maria Antiqua in the Roman Forum. Rome had become an outpost of Byzantine culture and mosaicists were called from abroad, and travelled far to carry out commissions in every part of the empire.

Pascal I (817–824) was no different from any earlier pope except that he was a lesser patron of the arts. However, three of the churches he built and their mosaics are still preserved. They are evidence of a revived Roman mosaic school that seems to have had a vital role in the renewed rise of religious art in the Christian West. This began after Pascal's papacy, and one of its products is the mosaic of around 800 which adorns the arch of the church of SS. Nereo ed Achille. Brilliant colours and the use of large glass tesserae relate this to the early Christian art of the past and are a mark of the mosaics of Pascal I. The Church of Santa Prassede may be taken as typical of Pascal's aims: as R. Krautheimer has shown, it was built in imitation of St Peter's with a transept and a large nave; the decoration emulates another great model in Rome: the mosaics of SS. Cosma e Damiano. Almost as a direct copy down to the detail of imagery and colour combination, the arch and the composition of arch and apse were repeated in Santa Prassede. Even the technique of the original reappears, with stained glass tesserae of fairly large cut. In the Lamb's halo and in the sheep frieze the silver of the original is copied, this being the only use of it in Roman mosaics before Charlemagne. Such precise copying is unmatched in medieval monuments. It was surely inspired by the Byzantine theology of icons: a sacred picture must copy the original in every least detail.

On page 53: St Peter's, Rome. *Christ as the Sun*, ascending to heaven in a chariot, surrounded by vine shoots. Mosaic in the vault of a mausoleum under the basilica (early fourth century A.D.). To the left at the base, where the mosaic has fallen, the painted preparatory plaster is visible.

Opposite and below: Piazza Armerina, floors of the Roman Villa Casale with scenes of *Hunting Beasts* and a personification of *Africa*. By African craftsmen, late third century.

On pages 56–57: Santa Costanza, Rome. *Grape Harvesting*, scenes from the vault (c. 330).

Below: Santa Pudenziana, Rome. *Christ enthroned* between the apostles and the personifications of the Gentile and Jewish Churches before Jerusalem. End of the fourth century. Extensive restoration work was carried out on the right-hand part and on the two figures to the right of Christ.

58

DOMINVS ECCLESIAE
CONSER PVDENTI
VATOR ANAE

Opposite and below: Aquileia, basilica. On the site of today's cathedral, Bishop Theodorus (d. 319) had built two halls for services, with a court in between for the baptistry. Both halls had richly adorned floors, the best preserved being that in the southern one, almost 750 sq m (8,000 sq ft), a vast rectangular area with the story of Jonah depicted inside a large marine scene, a detail of which is reproduced opposite, and three parts each containing three panels separated by decorative sheaves. In the central panel there are four busts of the Seasons and five portraits arranged in a cross which may show members of Constantine's family. These mosaics were carried out shortly after the death of Theodorus.

Below: Milan, San Lorenzo Maggiore, Chapel of St Aquilinus, *Christ the teacher among the apostles*. Mosaic in the east apse. Fourth century.

Opposite and below: Santa Maria Maggiore, Rome. *Abraham receives the three angels* (below, detail), and *Passage through the Red Sea*. Mosaics in the nave (435–440 A.D.).

On pages 66–67: inside the Mausoleum of Galla Placidia, Ravenna. At the back, St Lawrence (or, according to some sources, Christ Triumphant), the grid he died on and the chest with the books of the Gospel; above, two apostles (early fifth century).

On pages 68–69: Ravenna, Baptistry of
the Orthodox, cupola (449–452).

Below: Milan, Sant'Ambrogio, Chapel of
San Vittore in Ciel d'Oro. *St Felix, St
Maternus and St Nabor*, wall mosaic.

Opposite: *Glorification of St Victor*, center
of vault. Late fifth century.

Opposite: Ravenna, San Vitale, presbytery vault (c. 530).

Right: Ravenna, San Vitale. *St Luke.* Wall mosaic in the presbytery (c. 530). The mosaic scheme of the presbytery in San Vitale in Ravenna before the two panels with emperors, carried out around 457, was inspired by a merging of Old and New Testament scenes: the offerings of Abel, Melchisedek, and Abraham and the sacrifice of Isaac were forerunners of Christ's sacrifice; the law given to Moses foretold the New Testament of Jesus. The age of prophets and that of the Evangelists were merged by the suggestion of a landscape with rocks and meadows. San Vitale was begun by Bishop Ecclesius (521–534).

Right: Church of SS. Cosma e Damiano, Rome. Christ acclaimed by the apostles Peter and Paul, to whom Cosmas and Damian with St Theodore offer crowns, while Pope Felix IV presents the model of the church (c. 520), with the seventeenth-century restoration on the figure of the pope and the first three lambs on the left. The hand with the crown, at the top, has been recently restored. The apse of Cosmas and Damian was consecrated by Felix IV (525–530) and is regarded as the final example of Roman monumental art. Note a certain contrast between the vigorous shapes of the central group and the priestly aspect of St Theodore on the right. On the left, the figure of Felix IV is a seventeenth-century restoration.

Below: cupola of the Arian Baptistry,
Ravenna. Detail with St Peter and
St Paul before the Lord's throne
surmounted by the cross.

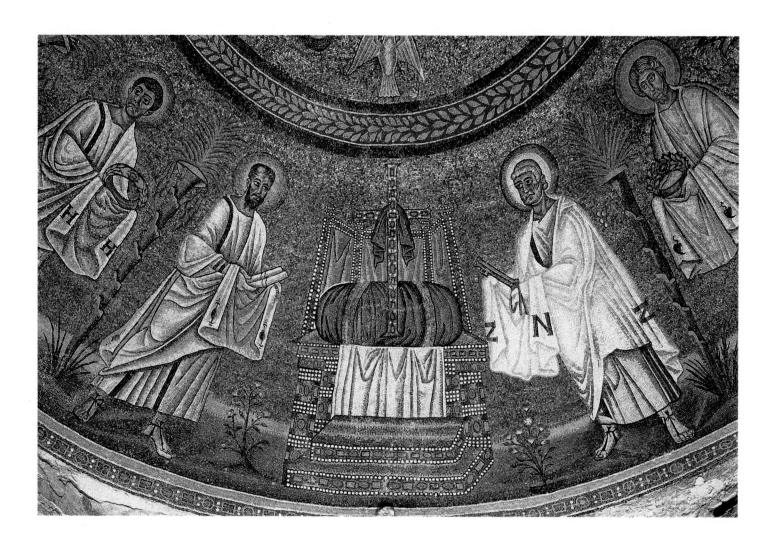

Below: cupola of the Arian Baptistry, Ravenna (after 493). The mosaics correspond to those in the Baptistry of the Orthodox, but are here strongly simplified. In the former the procession of apostles goes round a central theophany to which it pays homage, in the latter the procession moves towards the altar on which the cross is placed. The proclamation of the Divinity of Jesus in the Baptistry and his Passion are both visible to the baptized.

Left: San Vitale, Ravenna. *Justinian*, preceded by Bishop Maximianus and two deacons with gospel and incense, on his way to place a gift on the altar of the church (c. 547). Actually, the emperor never came to Ravenna.

Left: San Vitale, Ravenna. The Empress Theodora in the atrium of San Vitale, proceeding to the basilica bearing a gift, escorted by ladies of the court and two officials (c. 547). Like Justinian (see page 79), Theodora never came to Ravenna.

Below: San Vitale, Ravenna. *Royal Palace of Ravenna*, in Theodoric's time. The image of the Gothic king and his court were destroyed after the Byzantine reconquest. A few hands remain on the column shafts; note the forearm on the first column on the left. The figure of the ruler was placed in the area of gold at the center of the palace.

Opposite: presbytery of San Vitale, Ravenna. On the left, detail of a mosaic depicting the story of Moses (c. 530); on the right, mosaic showing the Emperor Justinian (c. 547).

Below: Sant'Apollinare Nuovo, Ravenna.
The Calling of Peter. This mosaic dates
from the time of Theodoric's reign.

Below: Sant'Apollinare Nuovo, Ravenna. *St Martin*. The church was erected by King Theodoric (493–526) and dedicated to the Saviour under the Arian cult. Although the apse mosaics were destroyed during eighteenth-century restoration work, there are wall mosaics in the nave including, in the upper area, twenty-six scenes of the miracles and Passion of Christ, and between the windows on each side, sixteen figures of prophets and patriarchs. The lower part contained, on one side, the king's palace and on the other the port of Classe with a procession on either side approaching the Virgin and Christ among angels. With the Byzantine reconquest, Bishop Agnello (556–569) substituted the figures of the two processions with saints and martyrs guided by St Martin, leader of the anti-Arian struggle.

85

Left: apse of Sant'Apollinare in Classe, Ravenna. St Apollinare praying below in the center. The sheep represent the apostles and the scene in the upper half of the apse symbolizes the Transfiguration (549).

SCA AGNES

Left: apse of Sant'Agnese, Rome. The saint stands at the center between the popes Sylvester I, founder of the basilica, and Honorius (625–638), who commissioned the mosaic.

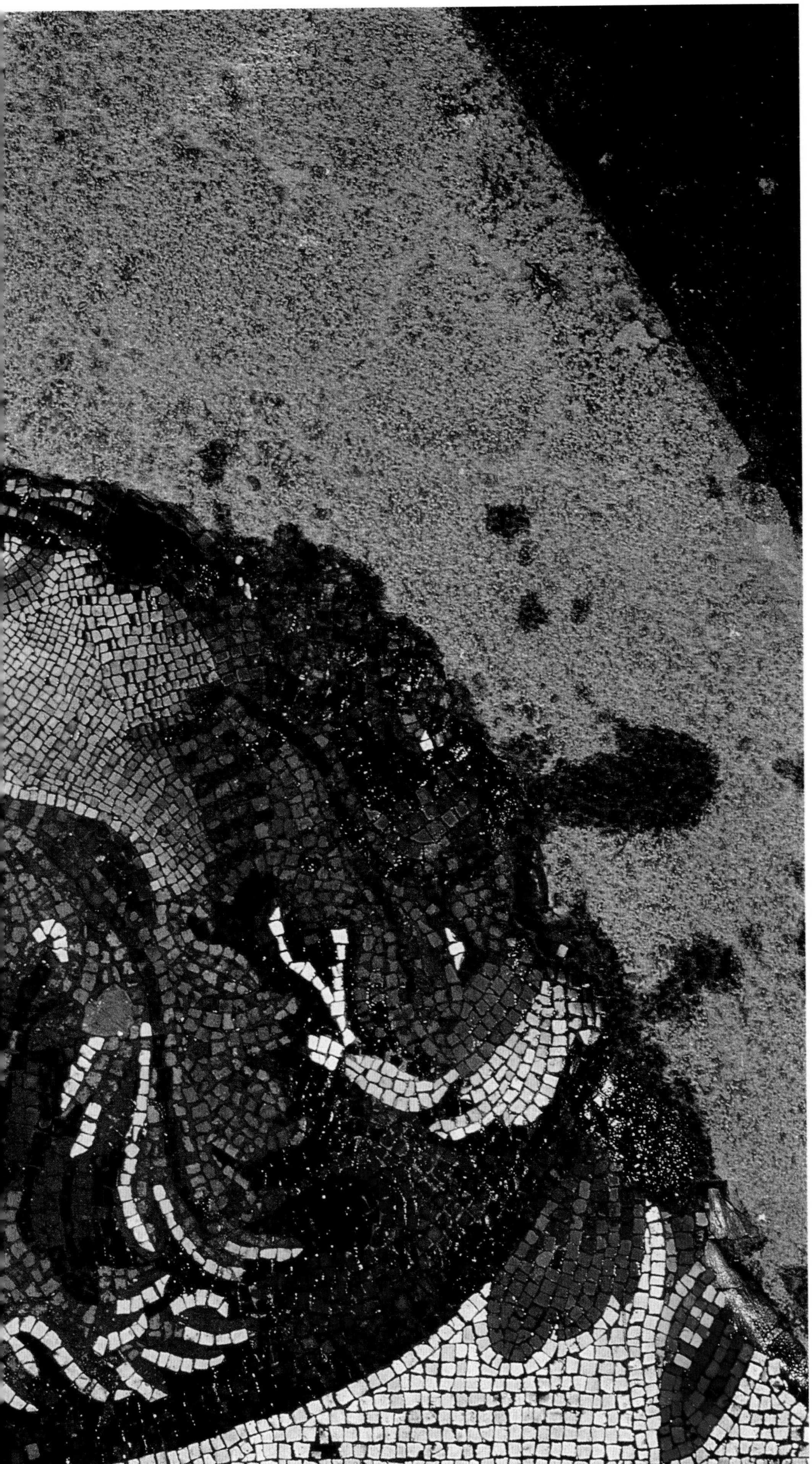

Left: *Mask* from the peristyle floor of the Royal Palace of Constantinople. Seventh century (?). Mosaic Museum, Istanbul.

Left: *Pastoral Scene* from the peristyle floor of the Royal Palace of Constantinople. Seventh century (?). Mosaic Museum, Istanbul.

93

Below: Santa Maria in Cosmedin, Rome. *Adoration of the Magi*, fragment of mosaics made for Pope John VII (705–707) in St Peter's.

Opposite: Santa Prassede, Rome. *Head of Saint*. Detail of mosaics carried out for Pope Pascal I (817–824) in the mausoleum of his mother (now Cappella di San Zeno).

Right: apse of Santa Prassede, Rome.
Christ acclaimed by St Peter and St Paul
on the banks of the Jordan (detail).
Commissioned by Pope Pascal II,
resuming the triumphal theme of the
church of SS. Cosma e Damiano.

Opposite: apse of Santa Maria in
Domnica, Rome (detail). The pope
kneeling before the Virgin is Pascal I
(817–824), who commissioned the
mosaic.

Right: apse of the Basilica of St Mark, Rome. Built for Gregory IV (824–844), it differs from the style of Pascal I.

On page 100: Santa Prassede, Rome. Vault in the mausoleum of Pascal I's mother. The motif of angels holding up the shield comes from Ravenna.

BYZANTINE TREASURES

Some great mosaics of the Eastern tradition have long been familiar to the worlds of art and academia, but only since the end of the 1950s has their history been pieced together. In the late nineteenth century, French and Russian scholars produced works on the great mosaics of St Luke's and Daphni churches in Greece and of Kahrie Djami in Istanbul, but a new world seemed to open in the 1930s, when Kemal Atatürk allowed the American scholar Thomas Whittemore to start restoring the Christian mosaics in the mosque of Aya Sofia, the ancient basilica of Hagia Sophia in Istanbul. The results were spectacular and their publication began in 1934. In the interwar years, the great mosaics going back to the first Arab rulers of Syria and Palestine were likewise studied. Since 1945 there has been a series of efforts to refurbish and restore monuments throughout the old Byzantine empire and neighbouring regions. In the early 1950s, began the cleaning and rediscovery of the fabulous early Byzantine mosaics of Salonika in Greece, as well as fragments of Palaeologus (late Byzantine) decorations of the same city. In the 1960s, a team of Egyptian and American experts did marvels in cleaning and preserving the sixth-century apsidal mosaic in St Catherine's monastery on Mount Sinai. At the same time, some Soviet scholars published works on the eleventh-century mosaics by mixed groups of Byzantine and Russian artists at Kiev, while in Italy the great medieval mosaics were studied afresh, in particular those of St Mark's in Venice, the baptistry of the cathedral in Florence and the great Norman churches of Sicily.

A prime result of Whittemore's work in Hagia Sophia, the largest Eastern Christian church, was to identify the part played by Justinian, the founder, in the decoration. He chose aniconic designs (using no images or idols), perhaps to emulate the great building of Solomon's temple in Jerusalem which was so alive in the minds and imagination of early Christians. Scholars who have examined the mosaics estimate that the golden "sky" in the vaults and domes of Hagia Sophia contains some one hundred and fifty million golden tesserae, one of the largest mosaics ever, using over one thousand tons of glass. Justinian's mosaics are severely simple, yet amazingly subtle and refined, as seen in the use of silver in the great vaults decorations and in the smaller checkered designs that cover the original parts of the dome. More spectacularly still, a new device enabled the golden tesserae mounted at the top of vertical walls or at poorly-lit points to keep their refractive power. The golden tesserae sparkling on the plane surface would have sent light rays into the space above the sight line, making the gold look opaque and polished. To focus the reflections directly on the viewer's eyes, the gilded tesserae, like hundreds of tiny mirrors, would have to be set at an angle towards the bottom. The Justinian portions of the mosaics in the narthex and nave have walls on which the tesserae are angled in this way. The resultant mirror effect mysteriously heightened the sheen produced by candle light at night. Even in daytime the gold was meant to sparkle: in a high corner of the narthex where the light is fairly dim, we observe how the artists have arranged the tesserae downwards or obliquely to catch the light from an adjacent window and direct it to the pavement much lower down.

The technique of angled tesserae may be a sixth-century invention, probably first used in the Church of St Polyeuktos in Constantinople, built 525–527; gold tesserae set obliquely in the plaster have been found in the rubble on the ruined site. Inclined cubes have been found in place in another ruined church about a decade older in Asia Minor. These are the oldest sources of evidence but a trace of the development lies in the Church of St George in Salonika, Greece. The date of the mosaics in this huge church remains disputed, but archaeological and iconographic evidence and the lack of haloes on saints make the date 380–90, originally proposed by H. P. L'Orange and by H. Torp, the most likely. In the reign of the emperor Theodosius, the building was changed from a mausoleum to a church, mosaics being added before the split of the Empire. Now considered as an early model for cupola decoration, as found in the Orthodox Baptistry in Ravenna, the Church of St George, which is rather larger than the Ravenna church, has a design in three large bands. Below the center, made up of a huge medallion carried by flying angels with a standing figure of Christ, unfolds a belt with at least thirty large figures of which only a few survived after the church became a mosque in the fifteenth century. These are the saints of the lower band which form a sumptuous architectural frieze divided into eight panels with, alternately, altars and baptismal fonts surmounted by ciboria and flanked with two saints whose names are inscribed near the heads.

This imposing set shows some quite new features in mosaic art. Foremost is the use of silver, treated with a mastery that suggests an established tradition. It is used in the background of the medallion round Christ and is found for the first time as a means to enhance the figure. Furthermore, stark silver rays are here widely used to intensify light. Except for some minor areas in which silver tesserae form intense patches to emphasize symbols of particular significance, such as the cross or baptismal water, the silver is blended with ordinary white tesserae to heighten their colour, for example in the white tunics of warrior saints.

Moreover, silver encroaches on the architectural background, where it mingles with gold to heighten the uncanny light emanating from the City of Heaven which it actually represents. On the architraves and cornices, silver appears as a source of light between golden tesserae, on the column shafts it runs in ordered vertical threads parallel to gold ones, and marks the line of maximum refraction. The turn to this level of illusionism, never seen before in the West, shows the impact of Eastern Christian painting where images do not just show stories and dogmas of faith, but rather attempt to embody them.

Another novelty is the light in the setting of faces and hands. Here is the first known example of natural stone used for those details, a feature that lasted throughout Byzantine mosaic art, for all of a thousand years. The saints' heads in the lower belt, and those of angels in the next, show what fine textural effect could be achieved in the late sixth century using the whole colour range of natural stone to create the soft transitions of skin colouring. Between six to eight colours are used, some in several shades, in a palette from milk-white to dark red-violet through a scale of pink and reds, not forgetting touches of pale yellow, and greenish-blue from marble cut in caves on islands of the Sea of Marmara, off Constantinople. The faces consist of tesserae smaller than those used for hair and clothes or the surrounding architectural elements; this too, with rare exceptions, went on for the whole Byzantine period. Mosaicists used the tesserae to "paint" faces. However, pieces just as small but strongly coloured were used for marked shadows and outlines. Areas of tiny glass tesserae in a fairly bright red are found at points of the strongest white light (again in marble). Here and there we find checkered shading, optically merging bluish-green glass with pink marble, for example, and alternating tesserae of two very different materials and colours. This device too was often used in later mosaics. It would be interesting to understand the reasons behind this strange use of materials and above all the notions that led to a coherent set of rules for representing the human face.

Natural stone is used for other ends as well. White marble is combined with white glass garments in a clearly expert play on structures, as seen in a later Western example: the white pallium of marble tesserae worn by Peter in the Arian Baptistry in Ravenna, which stands out from the normal pallia of glass tesserae worn by the other apostles, distinguishing the wearer of the sacred woollen pallium which remains a holy symbol of the pope in office. Deliberate choice surely dictated the use of natural stone for faces too, as craftsmen were inspired by the possibilities of illusionism. A similar development occurred with metallic tesserae, when, with the study of optics, the range of effects was realized.

It is the opaque surface achieved with stone that is the key to their use. It was to convey, through the grain of the material, the effect of a fine and translucent tissue lending authority to the sacred figures appearing on the walls of the church. They are no longer mere pictures, but become real.

Salonika, the second largest city in the Byzantine empire, has become a sanctuary of Christian mosaic art like Ravenna, such is the number of monuments preserved there. In 1917, much of the then recently discovered mosaics in the Church of St Demetrius perished in the great fire that destroyed the city. In the 1980s, earthquakes severely damaged St George and other churches, and restoration will take many years yet. The Church of St Demetrius, a large basilica with five naves, was decorated with frescoes and mosaics. Of the former, little remains; the fragments that just after the fire could still be seen high up in the nave are proof of the unusual decoration, the higher bands being painted and the lower in mosaic. During the Middle Ages, the church was damaged more than once, and the upper decorations were probably often renovated. Frescoes, involving less expense, seem to have replaced the original mosaics. Nearer to eye level, the walls were reserved for more personal worship in the form of countless ex-voto tablets offered by private members of the church. These valuable icons were always renewed or restored after each disaster. Many were salvaged from the fire of 1917.

A pale reflection of the splendour of the lost mosaics and their often moving message is conveyed by the interesting watercolours of the English architect and scholar W. S. George, painted some years earlier. Each of them centered on an aspect of St Demetrius, the holy warrior, shown frontally with his cloak over a tunic and black and white trousers. A full portrayal of the Virgin shows her in her role as protectress, enthroned and flanked by angels and saints. A donor, in miniature, stands up at the edge of the group, his hands respectfully covered by his cloak.

This panel is alongside a fascinating set of four paintings in which a lady presents her daughter named Maria to St Demetrius. The child, marked with a small golden cross on her forehead, is shown as in a cartoon, in various stages of her childhood. This gallery of mosaic icons in lively colours reflects the devotion which artists showed in their pictures, a basic feature of Byzantine piety from the sixth century on. In the panels high above the floor, the nimbus of St Demetrius consists of tesserae arranged at certain angles; in some cases the gold ones are positioned concentrically towards the central point of the head as well as downwards, which introduces depth, making the gold disks appear as if extended in space. In one case the saint is shown with hands of gold tesserae, literally his "golden hands" working miracles as Greek hymns often have it.

Christ's appearance, among the four beasts, to the apostles Peter and Paul on the waters of the Jordan is shown in the mosaic in the apse of St David, in colours rivalling those of fifth-century Italian mosaics. It has many refined touches, from the arabesques in quite separated tesserae which, as in St Demetrius, produce an almost other-worldly glimmer, to the extent of coloration in the silver streaks of the water course at the Saviour's feet and the shaping of the light blue god of rivers, the Jordan. On the triumphal arch the inscription is in silver on deep red, like the silver script on purple parchment of the most precious manuscripts.

Thanks to a wall that concealed them, the mosaics of St David survived the iconoclasts, when on the emperor's orders images were plastered over or destroyed. The ex-voto paintings in St Demetrius were saved because people put up resistance to the more violent forms of iconographic destruction, or perhaps they were left unharmed and on view because St Demetrius had assumed the role of the city's protector and was a national symbol. When the conflict (about 730–850) was over, restoration and redecoration began.

One example of this effort survives in the Church of Hagia Sophia, Salonika, where the mosaics in the cupola have an inscription that dates them to the turn of the ninth century. They show the Ascension with Christ in the center of the cupola; he sits in a medallion held high by angels while below the assembled apostles respond with expressive movements and gestures; the Virgin is in the middle of them, arms raised in prayer, flanked by angels. The design was conceived for a dome and allowed for its spherical shape to create the visual illusion. The dome becomes the stage on which the Ascension is performed, in a representation accurate even to its unfolding in space. Christ is poised high above the apostles who, in a stance adopted by the spectator looking from below and far off, have to stretch their necks to see Him.

Recent studies date the building to the seventh century; very likely the dome was decorated even then with an Ascension scene, and the invention of such theatrical effects belongs to pre-iconoclastic times. When in the late ninth century the scene was reintroduced, that phase was over. The time was ripe for a different Byzantine design, with Christ Pantocrator at the center of a cupola and the surrounding curved surfaces unfolding the whole hierarchy of Christian saints and heroes. This great new design was indeed based on the Ascension but made full use of architecture to render the mysteries of the faith visible in three dimensions.

Photographs of the saints taken from the galleries, and often reproduced, show strangely elongated and almost deformed bodies, because they are taken at an angle from which they should never be viewed. The correct perspective is that from directly underneath, where they appear normally proportioned, because the curvature of their positioning in the cupola is balanced by their elongation. This style is the highest point in the development of abstraction which began in Justinian's time and made a radical break with the Graeco-Roman past. We find it in the early ninth-century mosaics in Rome but only in the Byzantine case is it executed with the splendid technique developed in the East.

Among the prewar discoveries in Istanbul, the most amazing was a floor mosaic on the former site of the Great Palace of the Byzantine emperors. It was huge, some one thousand square meters of pavement in a covered passage round the four sides of a large courtyard, and made brilliant use of the technique and style of Roman-Hellenistic mosaic floors.

The themes were familiar, fights between men and beasts or between different species of animals, with more or less quiet, everyday scenes in between. This range of favourite Roman themes contained mythological animals too: the griffin, Chimera (composite of lion, goat and snake), and a faun with a child on his shoulders. Excavations under the mosaics revealed shell vases with incised crosses, clear proof that this work of pagan inspiration dates from after the advent of Christianity, about 400, may be from imperial circles. After the Second World War, excavation was resumed and new discoveries have shifted the dating to a later Christian era. Marks on bricks in the remains of an earlier building underneath were sixth century, and some capitals found in the earthwork under the pavement were of a type known to be seventh century. Moreover, it could be shown that the building as a whole was used as a basilica or audience chamber in the Palace and remained as such for centuries in medieval times before falling into ruin. The date thus seems late sixth century, and the work was attributed to a successor of Justinian. It could indeed be seventh or eighth century and represent a vital piece of evidence for evaluating one of the many "renaissances" that spread from Constantinople.

The Byzantine capital's role in art has been much discussed and contested. The "official Byzantine style" first appears in the sixth century in places as far apart as Ravenna and the Sinai desert. There, in the monastery of St Catherine rebuilt by Justinian at the foot of Mount Sinai, there is a famous apsidal mosaic showing full Byzantine refinement, with the use of angled tesserae for optical effect seen best in the medallions on the triumphal arch with busts of the Virgin and John the Baptist where the ground is of angled silver tesserae. The treatment of colour is masterly, especially in the Transfiguration in the apse, where the rays of light from Christ's mandorla are like flashes penetrating the church from outside.

The "renaissance" of the seventh century, through itinerant artists, reached the West (Rome), as seen in the mosaics of Pope John VII shortly after 700. In the East it managed to enter the alien world of expanding Islam. Greek painters decorated the hunting lodges of the caliphs, built in the desert, with unselfconscious classical nudes or with scenes showing the Arabs' triumph over their enemies.

The Mosque of Omar (or Dome of the Rock) in Jerusalem of the late seventh century and the Great Mosque of Damascus of the early eighth, have splendid mosaics by Byzantine artists. In the former, classicizing acanthus motifs mingle with those favoured by the Arab patrons such as stylized flowers and palms. In the darker areas of the building, gold tesserae are angled so that the view will embrace the sheen.

In the vast edifice of the Great Mosque not only the large hall of worship but also the walls of the court in front of it, some hundreds of meters long, have large mosaic friezes. The theme is a landscape unfolding over the whole length with rivers, rocks and villages. The technique shows it was the work of a large imperial workshop. The Byzantine empire, having contained the shock of attack by Islam from without and overcome the internal crisis of iconoclasm, rose to renewed splendour in political, material and artistic culture.

A new type of religious building arose that could be adapted to various uses, as palace chapel or modest parish church. Its most peculiar feature is the central cupola around which the rest of the building develops. In the most elaborate version, it has barrel vaults extending under the cupola in four directions to form a Greek cross with quite elaborate wings round it, sometimes with a large secondary cupola or small cupolas on the corners of the square of the plan. In a simplified version we have a small church like a chapel in which the cupola rests on four columns and forms a Greek cross, with a simple square space round it with apse attached. This solution became a model of excellence for Greek Orthodox churches and has been up to our own day.

The architecture of the new church needed mosaics and its curved surfaces (cupolas, vaults and numerous arches) were an ideal site for pictures needing a touch of spatial realism. Many indeed maintain that the buildings were put up as backdrop for images, and as such were so successful as to be later confirmed as canons.

The convent church of Daphni near Athens, built about 1100, is one of the foremost of such monuments. Its mosaics are largely intact, although much restoration work has been done. The inside follows a layout which, when compared to the wealth of detail adopted in early Christian art, seems very simple. At the center of the cupola there is a medallion with an enormous bust of Christ Pantocrator. In the lower part of the cupola, separated from the medallion by a large strip of gold, are the prophets with their scrolls. Lower still there must at first have been medallions with portraits of the evangelists.

In the four arches that support the cupolas there are scenes from the life of Christ which, with eight more such scenes in the transepts, formed a didactic cycle dedicated to the most important church festivals. The Virgin is shown in the apse, with her court of archangels on the side walls of the sanctuary. About thirty saints, shown wholly or in bust only, fill the remaining space. In the vestibule further scenes from the life of Christ unfold, as well as the remains of a cycle on the life of the Virgin. Golden cornices with floral ornaments surround the panels, and at one time the whole space between them was covered in gold. The whole is a picture of the Christian cosmos, whose effect is created by an intricate interplay between figures and architecture. The worshipper, moving inside this golden shell, could see the order of the world fitting perfectly into space. It is space that merges the whole decoration into a vast single image in which the Lord, venerated by the prophets surrounding Him, is in His sphere above the group of saints that inhabit the lower part.

The "classical arrangement" was probably perfected between 800 and 900, but the first examples extant go back to 1000–1100. Besides those at Daphni,

Greece has two other such monuments: the convent church of St Luke in Phocis and the Nea Moni of Chios, both eleventh century. Similar churches stand in far more distant places: St Sophia in Kiev (eleventh century) and the Martorana in Palermo (about 1150), both strongly Byzantine. The arrangement is, however, different in all of these. In the Nea Moni, the nave has very few figures, and St Luke has a big secondary cupola with a splendid picture of the Pentecost.

At Hagia Sophia in Constantinople, the abstract decoration was of course safe from the iconoclasts. Only some post-Justinian designs in smaller areas inside the building were slightly tampered with; though probably the apse had some figures, since some sources refer to a Virgin being destroyed. However, when the cult of images was resumed, the church was again splendidly adorned. Besides the Virgin in the apse, with the archangels at her side, on the large side walls of the nave were added the saints. The largest of these, of truly impressive size, are now lost, but they are remembered in a series of nineteenth-century drawings. They were to scale in relation to the space surrounding them. However, some of the smaller figures, brought to light by those assisting Whittemore, do seem very lost in space. The cupola almost certainly was decorated with a figure of the Pantocrator during the same period.

Two of the most beautiful mosaics executed when the church was redecorated are on the outer parts: one shows Constantine and Justinian flanking the Virgin and Child seated, the other a kneeling emperor adoring Christ enthroned. The technique in these late ninth-century works obeyed, without any sign of decadence, the violent interplay of colours and structures that had inspired pre-iconoclastic mosaics. Again, and at new peaks, we find the play of optical illusions. In the panel with the Virgin between the imperial donors, the Child Jesus seems to radiate light and in fact the golden garments that enfold Him are speckled with silver.

However, the "classical arrangement," while stressing the totality, gradually weakened the many spectacular effects of the earlier tradition in favour of balance and clarity of the whole. At Daphni, for example, the older mosaics are sumptuous like tapestry and use a sober range of colours less rich in shadings. The reds and yellows are limited, their function in the overall design being taken on by the gold of the ground. The blues, greens and violets, dark and often somber, are preferred to lighter tones. Like the mosaics of St Luke and Nea Moni, where the old colour scheme is more preserved (in the latter almost coarsely), those of Daphni seem cold and cerebral. This impression is further confirmed by the elegant style enriched with images from Classical art, sign of another "renaissance."

These mosaics actually belong to a new phase of Byzantine art called after the dynasty of the Comneni (1081–1185). This style reached its peak in Hagia Sophia at Istanbul on a panel in one of the galleries, showing the Virgin flanked by emperor John Comnenus II and his consort Irene.

Even the angling of tesserae seems to have been dropped, for it is absent in Daphni and in all mosaics of the classical style at its height. Silver was used merely to show the light emanating from God and Christ. This draining of luminous and colour effects was partly compensated for by the very precise joining and spacing of tesserae. The laws of visual perception were still of great importance.

The great Russian Byzantine scholar V. Lazareff, who studied the monuments of Kiev, reported that in eleventh-century mosaics in the local church of St Sophia one can see how carefully the master mosaicist had calculated the way of balancing the loss of strength at darker points where he used very intense pigment, so that the images might be seen through the shadows falling on them.

The "Paleologus renaissance" (after the Paleologus dynasty, 1261–1453) produced a renewal of Byzantine mosaic art. Fed by a vital humanism that spread to the West and contributed to the Italian Renaissance, painting reflected the need to obtain three-dimensional effects and a growing involvement in human feelings and actions. A nervous vitality entered religious art, along with a sense of pathos and tragedy.

In mosaic art this produced extraordinary results, with renewed techniques. Tesserae were usually smaller than before, and outlines became less rigid, softer and sometimes non-existent. Colour made these works once more very similar to early Christian mosaics, which may often have been used as models. There was renewed interest in the optical effects of gold, though rarely adopting the technique of angling the tesserae. On walls, the gold ground sometimes assumed the form of a shell, no doubt to heighten the play of surface light and to avoid too uniform a brilliance. In vaults, a close rib structure was preferred, which when covered with mosaic, produced reflections that spread to surrounding figures like rays from a central medallion.

Such vaults are preserved in Kahrie Djami, the former Church of Chora in Istanbul, rebuilt and decorated by way of devotional exercise by the logothete, or auditor, Theodore Metochites about 1315. Another amazing example is in Fetiye Cami (originally the church of St Mary Pammakaristos) in the same city.

A profound sense of colour, which is seen perhaps at its most refined in fragments of the decoration of the Church of the Holy Apostles in Salonika (about 1315) and at its highest intensity in the partly preserved cycles in Kahrie Djami, is what gives life to the supreme mosaic work of the panel of the Deesis in the south gallery of Hagia Sophia in Istanbul (about 1300). Here again tesserae are angled in the crossed arms of Christ's halo, confirming a hidden tendency of late Byzantine art to look back.

PORTATIVE MOSAICS

For about a century (726–843), with a short break (787–815), the Byzantine world underwent a crisis, the Iconoclastic Controversy, when a division arose between those who wanted a cult of icons and those who wanted to suppress it. The emperor supported the latter, giving them the power to proceed legally against those who still wished to venerate images of Christ, the Virgin or the saints, and the opportunity to set about destroying any portrayal of figures in churches, be they portable icons, frescoes or mosaics. The iconoclast party felt bound to lead Faith back to its early purity, condemning superstition and the interests (partly material) that flourished round the cult of sacred images. Meanwhile, others felt just as strongly that venerating them was an essential act of faith in the incarnation of the Word, and in its lasting efficacy through the acts of the apostles. To paint the figure of Christ was a privilege the incarnation had granted the faithful. To refuse to do it and refuse or fail to venerate images was therefore to deny that the incarnation was true. For the Byzantines, the icon was a direct product of its prototype, incarnating the essential qualities, rather than being an arbitrary or spontaneous creation. Through venerating the icon they would rise directly to Christ and the saints, whose essence was at the same time present in the icon itself.

Whether or not there were to be images in religious buildings or any other place of prayer was therefore no longer a simple matter of choice. In fact, during the short break in the iconoclastic struggle, it appears that images were even placed where they had never been before. This is what happened in Hagia Sophia in Constantinople, the great Justinian church which affirmed the orthodoxy of the whole empire. It was dedicated to the Divine Wisdom, a theme which proved hard to depict in images. Soon after 787 a large mosaic was added to the vault of its main apse, showing the Mother of God enthroned with her Son between two archangels. The fear had clearly been that adoration of the Divine Wisdom in an abstract form, without support of an image of the Logos incarnate, might not suffice to clarify the Orthodox faith as practiced in the basilica.

In the post-iconoclastic Byzantine world the icon therefore was ubiquitous. It no longer belonged to everyday experience in the unconscious forms of ascetic or popular religious behaviour of earlier times, but was a constantly repeated declaration of faith. In the imperial palace orthodox emperors during official receptions opened the resplendent *Chrysotriklinion*, the great hall with numerous apses sparkling with silver and gold, where the treasure of the *Pentapyrgion* was found and from which occasionally icons to be exhibited when foreign embassies arrived were extracted. These were objects to be admired for their rich beauty, but also as declarations of faith.

In modest churches, too, icons multiplied. They covered not only the sanctuary screen but also appeared everywhere, on walls as well as on special lecterns, *proskynetaria* or *analogia*. Since icons were not considered as inert pictures but as living things in which resides part of the inherent quality of the prototype, they were not left on the *proskynetarion* all the time, but covered and stored, then re-exhibited, depending on the run of the liturgical year. As the occasions for personal contact between worshipper and icon increased in Byzantine churches, there was a search for ways to denote intimacy in various relations in space and time. On the walls and at the top of the screen, the pictorial story of Christ and on the church door the Dormition of the Virgin, enabled one to run through the cycle of the liturgical year, while the movement of icons on the *proskynetaria* and the alternation of candles and flowers on each one gave a sense of the months and their saint days passing by.

The large dimensions did not favour the link of devotee to image that marked the Byzantine religion, and in the small vaults of churches covered in mosaics of the Paleologus age, as in the church of St Mary Pammakaristos in Constantinople, the smaller format of the icon, sometimes narrative and then gently spiritual, seems to prevail over the tradition of the monument itself. From Pammakaristos (today Fetiye Cami), built in the twelfth century by John Comnenus and his wife Anna Doukaina, comes a mosaic icon probably older than the church itself, now kept in the Orthodox patriarchate of Istanbul. It is a tablet (60 × 85 cm [2 × 2¾ ft]) showing the Virgin and Child in the Hodegetria style (a Byzantine design where the Virgin holds the Christ on her left arm and He is gazing forward almost unaware of His mother). It has often been compared in style with the mosaic on the same subject in St Sophia in Kiev, probably of the same period (eleventh century). Otto Demus has stressed that the resemblances between them go beyond general features of style: "The tesserae of the Constantinople icon are smaller than those in the Kiev one, but they are placed in the same curved patterns that define the form and give it its plastic force."

However, the technique in these and other Byzantine mosaics is not the same as in wall mosaics. Their support is always a hollowed wooden tablet with a raised edge. On this panel, usually cut with crossed lines for better adhesion of materials, a bed of wax and resin is prepared into which the small mosaic cubes are pressed. These included coloured stones, sometimes hard like lapis lazuli or malachites, marbles and glass tesserae. Gold is not usually in tesserae form but rather as a sheet of silver foil cut into regular pieces, usually rectangular. Gold was used rarely, as in such small quantities it is hard to handle, while silver could be covered with a varnish to simulate gold. The size of mosaic icons varies; the largest are close in kind to wall mosaics and came earlier, but in the Paleologus era large ones are still found, such as the famous *Virgin Glykophilousa* (the sweetly loving) in the Byzantine museum in Athens which is from St Basil of Triglia in Bithynia, dating from the early fourteenth century and measuring 95 × 62 cm (3 × 2 ft). On the other hand, the highly delicate icon of St Nicolas in the monastery of St John the Baptist on Patmos, which measures 14 × 10 cm (5½ × 4 in), seems to go back to the eleventh century. There may have been countless reasons for making icons bigger or smaller, but certainly mosaic icons were always held to be very valuable objects. In many cases they are set in silver cornices but in no case are they even partly covered with gold or silver foil; this variation in treatment shows that they were viewed differently from other icons. In many cases it is worth looking at the features of their history that made them objects of such particular value: the difficulty of technique, the colour inherent in the material itself (an admiration echoed in Ennodius's poems in the sixth century), their diminutive size (almost in miniature), with a technique considered monumental.

Admiration of the small mosaic icon with the dead Christ on the sarcophagus in the Roman basilica of Santa Croce in Gerusalemme gave rise to the legend that St Gregory had made it from bone fragments of martyrs. This tradition in turn became attached to the Carthusian one that St Gregory had celebrated a famous mass before this image, so freeing many souls from purgatory. This tale greatly influenced fifteenth-century painting, but the mosaic did not reach Rome till 1380, having been made in Constantinople early in the century whence it probably first went to Sinai. The magnificent diptych of the Opera del Duomo in Florence (each wing is 27 × 17.7 cm [10½ × 7 in]) was given to the Basilica of San Giovanni in 1395 by the noble Venetian Nicoletta di Antonio Grioni, widow of a councillor of the Emperor John Cantacuzenus, chased from the throne in 1354 by his son-in-law John Palaeologus and forced to become a monk. The icon very likely was part of the imperial treasure, perhaps to be exhibited in the *Chrysotriklinion*, and datable to before 1354.

The icon with Christ Pantocrator in the treasury of the collegiate church of Chimay, also early fourteenth century, was a gift from Sixtus IV to Charles de Croy, prince of Chimay. The elegant icon of St Demetrius now in the civic museum of Sassoferrato, in which mosaic technique rivals enamel-work in its scope to lend rare decorative weight to a repeated geometric motif, belonged to the humanist Niccolò Perotti (1429–1480). Its rich silver cornice with its double-headed Paleologus eagles shows that it came from the world of the court. Considering that donors often lived long after the icon's date, the sometimes much later silver cornices and the evidence that many of them have been subsequently repaired attest that these icons were highly esteemed. It has even been supposed that they were all made at Constantinople under some monopoly or imperial control, but this fits ill with the differences in style. While some are documented as clearly originating from Constantinople, other centers may well have managed more or less to imitate the technique from a model. If we consider the images not clearly assignable to Constantinople, made by lesser or provincial workshops, it is possible to compile a classification that takes these variations into account rather better.

An example is the dramatic dead Christ in the monastery of Tatarua, in Eurythania, which was conceived in terms of a heroic contrast between the large masses of muscle, the fine facial features and the huge helmet of hair, pierced by streaks of light. It was made by a great fourteenth-century artist, but along different lines from the makers of a group of Constantinople icons including a St Chrisogonus at Dumbarton Oaks, a St Theodore in the Vatican Library (Museo Sacro) and a Theodor Stratelates in the Hermitage, Leningrad. All these show the same feature of very gentle passages in the shading and minute tesserae (1 mm square and less) merging to give the impression of a unified painted surface. By contrast, golden light is spread over the whole like precious specks set on a transparent plane resting on the painted surface, while the design of geometric motifs in garments, haloes and cornices contrasts with the pictorial illusion of flesh. Similarly the gold ground tends to remain uniform and subtracts from the tension created by the outline of figures. In the Vatican icon, the subtle resolution of the mosaic components constantly returns from gold to colour, from one plane to another, as the eye gradually goes from the shield in the background to the lance in the foreground and runs along the yellow, red and black carpet on which the saint steps in his black half-boots with golden laces. The St Demetrius of Sassoferrato is later, when these first essays have already become mannerisms.

Alongside the pictorial icon group showing a single saint there are others with intricate scenes, such as the Florence diptych mentioned above and the stirring *Annunciation* in the Victoria and Albert Museum in London. In both, the intimate and fantastic tendencies of Byzantine painting at the time of the mosaics and frescoes of Kahrie Djami (early fourteenth century) find their equivalents. This is not a reduction to small size of compositions from another context, since the quality of these works lies precisely in the recovery of a certain impressionist disdain of late antique mosaic, through a contrast between the relative sizes of tesserae and the smallness of the detail to be captured. Viewed through a magnifying glass, some apostles' faces in the Florence *Dormitio Virginis* recall fourth-century fresco figures in the Hypogeum of the Via Latina in Rome, except that they are softer and more refined. Compared with the first cited group of icons, the Florence one has gold lights that seem to adhere to the images more, with the aim to highlight them rather than to superimpose them. An example of this way of treating lighting as an independent element, which successfully incorporates a more fused chiaroscuro effect at the same time, is found in the *Forty Martyrs* at Dumbarton Oaks, an absolute masterpiece of icon mosaic art, probably dating a little earlier than the Florence diptych.

When Constantinople fell, or perhaps even before, interest in work of such refinement must have been completely lost. However, these works were much admired in Italy, not only by collectors but also by artists. According to Vasari, Gaddo Gaddi went to great lengths to produce inexpensive substitutes for them, made of bits of shell which he glued on a tablet and coloured. Cennino Cennini, pupil of Agnoli Gaddi, gave a precise account of this technique, which he considered to be "mosaic or Greek work." This leaves it open to suppose that in the late fourteenth century, the great era of the portative mosaic we have looked at was replaced by a lesser one, in which mosaics were made with rather cheaper and less durable materials.

On page 113: Church of St George, Salonika. Vault of one of the eight niches carved into the walls. Only three retain their mosaic decoration, probably coeval with that of the cupola.

Below: Bet She'an (Israel), floor mosaic. The Jerusalem Talmud was completed around 425, and the Babylonian one around 500. The Talmud ("instruction") dictates the Laws, especially juridical ones, that regulate the life of Jewish communities. The Byzantine era up to the Arab conquest of 640 is therefore called "of the Second Talmud," marked in Palestine by a mushrooming of synagogues alongside the growth of Christian churches. In the early fourth

century, the rabbi Abun had introduced the use of floor mosaic. The synagogue of Bet She'an (sixth century) has a large panel with the menorah and various liturgical objects, now in the Museum of Israel in Jerusalem. In the frieze there are charming scenes and figures. Mosaics in synagogues of this period often feature numbers of people, the human figure being admissible provided it was not the object of a cult.

Below: Church of St David, Salonika.
Christ among symbols of the
Evangelists, adored by Elijah and Enoch,
over the mountain of Paradise whence
flow four rivers.

Left: Church of St David, Salonika. Detail of the preceding mosaic; in the foreground the lion, symbol of the Evangelist Mark. The heavenly appearance moves even nature, seen here in the figure representing the sea near the mountain, with its gesture of wonder.

On pages 118 and 119: Church of St George, Salonika. *Saints' faces.* Former imperial building of 293–311, converted into a church by the Emperor Theodosius late in the fourth century. Personages depicted in attitudes of prayer surround the lower part of the cupola.

Left: The apse of the Church of the Virgin in St Catherine's Monastery, Mount Sinai. Apse depicting the *Transfiguration*. The church was built by Justinian. The mosaic is representative of the final phase of Justinian art (550–565).

Below: Church of St Demetrius, Salonika. *Two parents present their son to St Demetrius.* The saint is depicted with golden hands. Seventh century.

Right: Church of St Demetrius, Salonika.
St Demetrius with two children. Votive
mosaic on a column.

Opposite: Church of St Demetrius, Salonika. *The Founder Bishop.* Detail of the mosaic dedicated to the founders of the church, shown flanking the saint who embraces them.

Below: Hagia Sophia, Istanbul. *Archangel* in the arch before the apse. The apsidal mosaics stand out from all known Byzantine monumental painting. They are commonly dated 867, in reference to a homily of the patriarch Photius, though some suggest the period 787–815 when legislation against images was suspended.

Below and opposite: Church of St Sophia, Salonika. *Angel*, and head of the *Virgin* (opposite), both details from the *Ascension* in the vault, which illustrates the renewed use of monumental painting after the ban on images. The three metallic elements near the angel are supports applied during an old restoration.

Below and opposite: St Luke, Phocis.
Below, medallion with the Virgin, St
John the Baptist and two archangels.
Opposite, above, apse with *Virgin and
Child*; below, detail of cupola with the
Pentecost. From 943 to 953, the blessed
Luke lived on the site of today's convent
dedicated to him. Here he founded a
first church. After he died (1011),
another, larger church was begun, with
mosaics that give us a coherent view of
Byzantine art in the early eleventh
century.

Opposite and below: Hagia Sophia, Istanbul. Lunette over the southwest door. Justinian, emperor "whose praises should be sung," offers the church to the Virgin and Child, while Constantine, "the great emperor amongst the saints," offers the city of Constantinople. Opposite, detail.

On pages 132–133: Hagia Sophia, Istanbul. Lunette over the Royal Entrance. The *Emperor Leo IV* prostrate before Christ enthroned. This act of humility may have been due to ecclesiastical doubts about the rather numerous marriages of the emperor, who died in 912.

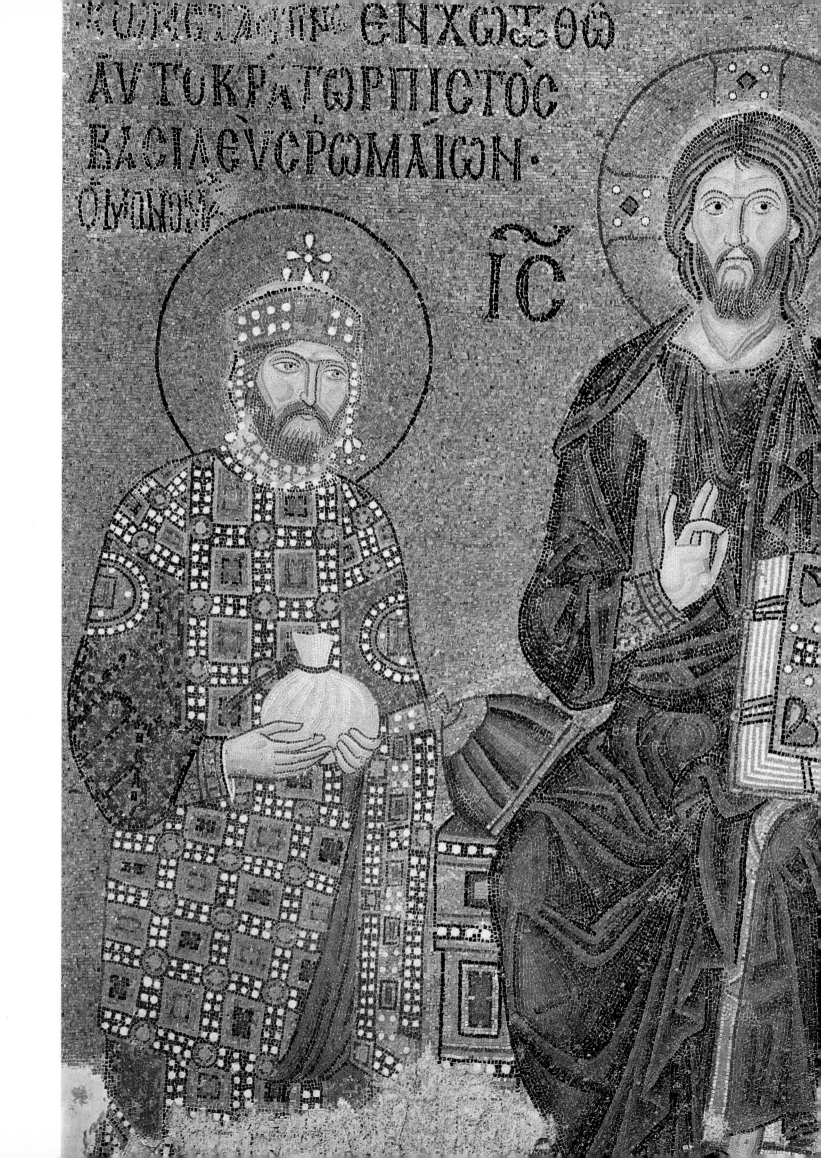

ΚωΝϹΤΑΝΤΙΝΟϹ ΕΝ ΧΩ ΤΩ Θ͞Ω
ΑΥΤΟΚΡΑΤΩΡ ΠΙϹΤΟϹ
ΒΑϹΙΛΕΥϹ ΡΩΜΑΙΩΝ ·
Ο ΜΟΝΟΜΑ

Ι͞C

Left: Hagia Sophia, Istanbul. *Christ enthroned*, Emperor Constantine Monomachus and his wife Zoë bringing Him gifts. She had married Constantine in 1042, so that his name and face replaced a previous husband. The portrait of Zoë, who was then about sixty years old, was likewise redone.

135

Below: Hagia Sophia, Istanbul. *Virgin and Child*, with Emperor John II Comnenus and his wife Irene (daughter of Ladislav of Hungary) bringing gifts (c. 1118).

Below: cupola of the monastery, Daphni, Attica. The eleventh-century mosaics represent an example of perfect harmony between architecture and imagery.

Below: monastic church at Daphni,
Attica. *The kiss of Judas*. On page 140:
detail.

140

Left: church at Daphni, Attica.
Presentation of Mary at the Temple. On
page 141, detail. The church at Daphni is
dedicated to the Dormition of the Virgin:
the mosaics also show *Scenes from the life
of Mary.*

144

Opposite and below: Hagia Sophia, Istanbul. *Deesis*, in the south gallery (probably after 1264). Opposite, detail of the Virgin.

Left: Hagia Sophia, Istanbul. Detail of *Deesis* with Christ and St John.

Below: Kahrie Djami (formerly the church of the monastery of Chora), Istanbul. Cupola of narthex. The name of the mosque (*djami, cami*) distorts the original one of the church it has replaced: Chora, Greek for country or land. The mosaics have transformed the place name by writing alongside the images: Christ, land of the living; the Mother of God, place of the unlimited, namely God (*Chora tou achorontou*). The church is twelfth century with fourteenth-century additions. Few interior mosaics remain, but most of those in the inner narthex are preserved, with *Scenes from the life of the Virgin*, and the outer narthex with *Scenes from the life of Christ*. Dedicated in 1320–21.

Opposite: Kahrie Djami, Istanbul. *Entry on the list of contributors*, detail from the *Scenes from the life of Mary*.

Below: Kahrie Djami, Istanbul. *Christ healing the lame.*

Opposite: Kahrie Djami, Istanbul. Second field in the outer narthex. To the left, *St John the Baptist announcing the coming of Jesus;* to the right, in clockwise direction, the *Temptations of Christ* on top of the temple, on the mountain, the kingdoms and the stones.

Below and opposite: cupola of Fetiye
Cami, Istanbul. Formerly church of St
Mary Pammakaristos (Full of Grace). As
at Daphni, Christ the Almighty (detail
opposite) is shown among the prophets
but he appears high and distant, while
the ribs of the cupola spread golden light
all round (c. 1310).

Below: Fetiye Cami, Istanbul. *St Gregory of Armenia*. One of the mosaics in the small side niches of the church (c. 1310).

Opposite: Church of the Holy Apostles, Salonika. *Transfiguration*, mosaic of 1310–1314.

Left: detail of *The Pantocrator*, mosaic icon in the Bargello Museum, Florence. Made in Constantinople (mid twelfth century); 54 × 41 cm (1¾ × 1¼ ft).

Opposite: portative mosaic icon, *Transfiguration*, made in Constantinople, late twelfth–early thirteenth century; 56 × 36 cm (1 ft 10 in × 1 ft 2 in). Musée du Louvre, Paris.

Below: the Greeks call icons of the Virgin embracing the Child "eleusa"; this mosaic icon is highly sentimental and dates from the late thirteenth century. Benaki Museum, Athens.

Opposite: *Dead Christ*, in an early fourteenth-century mosaic from Constantinople. "King of Glory" is inscribed in gold letters on the cross and is the name of this kind of Byzantine image. The cornice with the arms of Angio and Orsini del Balzo, goes back to about 1385, when the icon (13.3 × 8.4 cm [5½ × 3¼ in]) was given to the Roman basilica Santa Croce in Gerusalemme, where it is now.

On page 164: left wing of a mosaic diptych in the Opera del Duomo museum in Florence. The two wings show twelve *Scenes from the life of Christ* (each 17.7 × 27 cm [7 × 11 in]). Late fourteenth century.

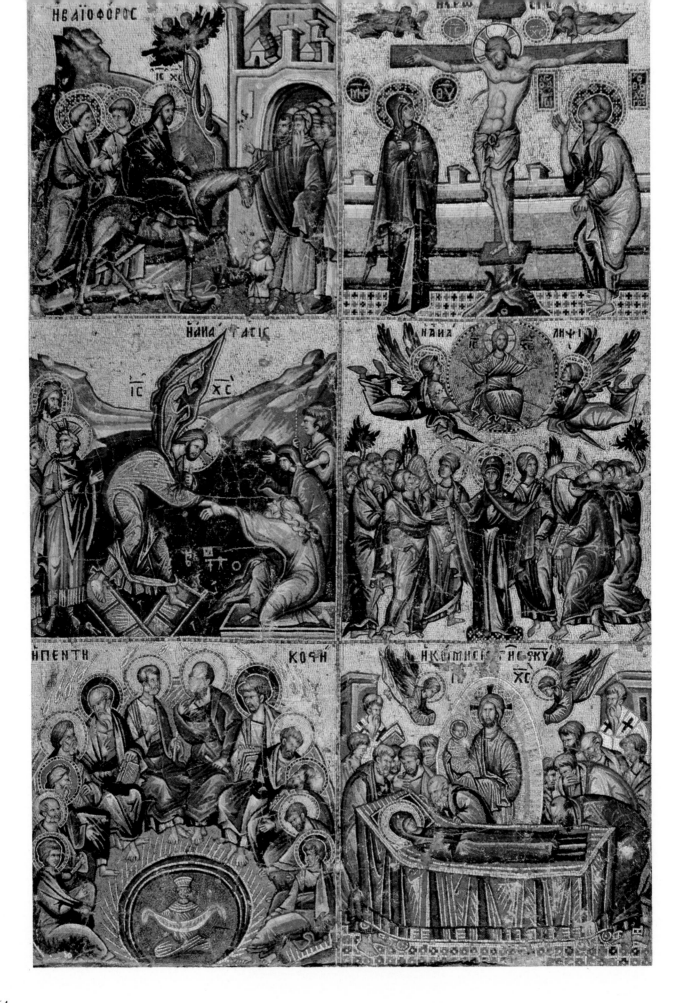

MOSAIC VAULTS
AND FLOORS IN ISLAM AND
THE WEST

Medieval buildings have mosaic decorations that remain in the tradition of late antiquity. With regional differences and variants in time depending on the survival of workshops and the demands of clients, mosaic in its two main forms, floor and wall, was to continue on its eternal course through the Middle Ages.

The technique differs in the two forms. As in antiquity, both are obtained by joining cubes of stone or marble (tesserae) set on a prepared surface. The variety in colour usually constituted the most striking feature. In pavements, marble slabs often alternate (in *opus sectile*) with mosaic work in tesserae. In such cases the materials are hard and need a final smoothing or polishing. During the Middle Ages wall mosaic was different from both floor mosaic and wall painting. What removed it from the latter was its plasticity, due to the technique of setting which was uneven and to the tesserae materials which were often different, making use of various types of glass and gold-leaf work. The variety in material is not a peculiarity of medieval times. Mosaic, far from imitating wall painting, had always produced effects of light and depth un-equalled by any other decorative technique. However, medieval mosaic was not simply an independent form of art, but above all one of the types of luxury decoration preferred by the wealthiest part of society. It adorns not only churches but also magnificent houses and castles. Extant examples of civic mosaic decorations are few, although we know they existed. For instance, of the wall mosaics in the Norman Royal Palace in Palermo there is a beautiful poetic account (early twelfth century) by Boudri de Bourgueil at the behest of Adele of Blois, daughter of William the Conqueror, proof that civic residences had mosaic floors even in Romanesque times. The iconography of this floor, presenting a large map of the world, shows how carefully the client chose the images. Immortalized on floor and walls, they formed part of the general corpus of medieval buildings. It is interesting to note how mosaics played a similar role in Romanesque, Gothic and Islamic art.

After the great mosaic works of Ravenna and Rome had flourished and spread in the fifth and sixth centuries, Western wall mosaic continued steadily though perhaps more restricted to Rome itself. Although in only a small number, Rome has examples of early Middle Ages mosaic adorning new religious buildings or earlier adapted ones. Elsewhere, the few examples to be found are very similar to the Byzantine and Italian models. The mosaic in the small oratory of a privileged subject of Charlemagne's court, Theodolfus, at Gemigny-des-Prés, between Orléans and Saint-Benoît-sur-Loire, is proof of how, in the late eighth century in Gaul, mosaic was still a possibility for the decoration of a private chapel. Wall mosaic is also linked with power in its own way throughout the Middle Ages. The mosaic in the cupola of the palace chapel of Aachen bears witness to the technical brilliance of Carolingian artists and to the way their clients linked this technique with the Italy of late antiquity. We know of this item through a drawing reproduced by Ciampini, a seventeenth-century scholar, since the mosaic itself was destroyed in the early eighteenth century.

The Roman basilicas of Santa Costanza, Santa Pudenziana, Santa Maria Maggiore and SS. Cosma e Damiano recall the brilliant mosaics of late antiquity that medieval artists in Rome had before them. They may have inspired the renewal of early Christian art in twelfth-century Rome, via the early medieval phase represented, for example, by the mosaics of Santa Prassede, Santa Susanna and SS. Nereo ed Achille. However, this Roman tradition is not enough to explain the sudden flowering of mosaic art in Rome. The famous abbey of Monte Cassino is the most obvious example, but we cannot enjoy it because the decoration of the basilica, carried out by artists called from Byzantium by the Abbot Desiderius, has been lost. A reflection of it probably remains in the elements of the first mosaic decoration preserved in the Cathedral of Salerno. Clearly wishing to identify with late antiquity, in outlook, politics and culture, Roman church patrons from 1100 demanded a renewal of mosaic technique which appears in two great examples: the apses of

San Clemente and of Santa Maria in Trastevere. The wall mosaic in the apse and triumphal arch of San Clemente exhibits a rich pictorial range on a background of acanthus leaves and branches that represent the Lord's vine, as the inscription along the base testifies. The decoration has many references to early Christianity. The twelve doves adorning the central cross and symbolizing the apostles correspond to a Paleochristian idea that is here enriched by the motifs of the Tree of Life and the Crucifixion. The small groups of people in the foliated scrolls are also ancient references and are in contrast with the formal structure of the large figures shown on the triumphal arch. The mosaic in San Clemente was completed between the years 1115–1125, while that in the apse of Santa Maria in Trastevere belongs to 1140–1143, during the episcopate of Innocent II. In aim it differs little from the former: standing figures flanking a central one are indeed common in late antiquity or early medieval Roman basilicas, as are the more apocalyptic features such as the inclusion of candelabra. However, the central image of the Virgin Crowned and Christ in Majesty on a big double throne is new: His hand is on His mother's shoulder, presenting her at the center of the saints facing the observer. However, the prominent position and larger dimensions belong to Christ, while the Virgin for a while longer occupies an inferior place. If the central group in the apse of Santa Maria in Trastevere concerns the Roman festival of the Ascension, as comparison with older icons suggests, this would give us a further hint for finding the sources and means of mosaicists who revived the old technical tradition round 1100. Pictorially, we need only consider the abyss that separates the mosaic of Santa Maria in Trastevere from the later one in Santa Maria Maggiore.

Almost at the same time as these, the wall mosaics of medieval Sicily underwent change dictated by very different stylistic sources and with quite other aims. After the Norman conquest of Sicily, the new princes soon revealed their ambitions in monumental decorations. In the era of Roger II (1105–1154), William I (1154–1166) and William II (1166–1189), Sicilian art was influenced by East and West alike. Their Norman origins were soon balanced by Eastern and Byzantine influences. Artists from Byzantium realized impressive schemes creating a true Sicilian school at Palermo, Monreale and Cefalù. The oldest mosaics can be confirmed from the inscription at the base of the cupola in the Cappella Palatina in Palermo to the date 1143. These mosaics in the eastern part of the chapel were probably the work of artists from Constantinople who came in 1140–1150. Also in 1143 the decoration in the small church of La Martorana, founded by George of Antioch, seems to have been completed.

To this first period belong the mosaics of Cefalù (an inscription gives the date of 1148). The three works were commissioned by Roger II, after he had established his rule. The mosaics follow Byzantine pictorial themes based on the Old and New Testaments, on the lives of the saints and on certain individual scenes. The Norman princes adapted these themes to their own ends, with glorious representations and unequivocal dedications. At La Martorana, the Christ dominates the cupola, surrounded in the vaults by four angels and in the drum by prophets and apostles. A cycle on the childhood of Christ gives the necessary story to link the start of the New Testament with the life of the Virgin. This cycle becomes more Christ-centered in the Cappella Palatina, but the two decorations are still alike in concept and execution. The links between liturgical and temporal power are summarized in an equally simple way in the portrait of Roger II crowned by Christ in La Martorana in Palermo. A clear parallel with imperial Byzantine scenes, Roger II in the emperor's robes receives the crown from the hands of Christ.

The decoration of the Cathedral of Monreale in Sicily brings new Byzantine air in the late tenth century. One of the largest medieval decorations, it is a vital point of reference for Byzantine painting round 1180–1190. It is the great work of William II's time. Working from the apse of the Cathedral of Cefalù, the artists of Monreale produced an arrangement in three levels. The scene in the middle one does not show the Virgin standing as in Cefalù, but seated with the Child in her arm in a prominent position directly under the commanding bust of the Pantocrator. Archangels and saints complete adornments in the apse. The nave, in more narrative style, shows scenes from the Old Testament in a manner found elsewhere in older Sicilian decorations.

Sicily also has outstanding examples in the decoration of princely houses. The so-called Norman chamber of King Roger, actually from the time of William I, in the Royal Palace in Palermo preserves mural scenes that bear witness to the melting-pot of cultures, languages and religions there from 1150–1200. The walls are adorned with hunting scenes and animals shown frontally, standing out from a background of exotic trees in stiff, linear style, no longer Byzantine but mainly late ancient. On the whole, such examples were close to magnificent floor mosaics from which the artists could draw inspiration, given that in the twelfth century the area still had some villas from late antiquity. It has also been revealed that images on cloth or on Islamic objects inspired medieval mosaic art. The pavilion of La Zisa, in a large park south of the city, has a mosaic similar to those in the Palace of Palermo, with the same decorative themes of geometric designs and symmetrical figurative scenes that are once again inspired by late antiquity but with Islamic touches. The weight of Islamic culture in Sicily is displayed particularly in these private decorations, in contrast with the Byzantine rigour of wall mosaics in religious buildings. The Islamic luxury of the architecture and above all the imposing decorations do not seem to have a corresponding mosaic tradition in Islam.

It is interesting to note at this point that the Umayyads (the ruling dynasties of Damascus, 661–750 and later in southern Spain, 756–1031) adopted tessera mosaic at a time when late ancient mosaic technique was still in use, especially in the Eastern Mediterranean. The discovery of mosaics in various princely houses, particularly one at Khirban al-Mafjar in Jordan, with plant and animal decorations, shows how well these princes were integrated into Byzantine culture even on an iconographic level. The cupola of the Dome of the Rock in Jerusalem, the Mosque of El-Aksa and the Great Mosque of Damascus retain richly decorated eighth-century wall mosaics. The cupola of the first has very elegant fronds that seem to burst forth from vases and acanthus tufts, to the point of covering the free space in the corners of the arcades. In the portico of the Great Mosque of the Umayyads in Damascus the decoration unfolds views of country houses and villages standing out at the center amongst big trees in truly Hellenistic style, perhaps even Alexandrian. Such landscapes go back to a late ancient tradition and are rare in Islamic art. Similarly we could consider other aniconic images such as those of the Councils in the nave of the Church of the Nativity, Bethlehem, and compare all these with other non-Islamic Eastern decorations. In the West, the mosaics of the Mosque of Cordova show that Islamic southern Spain adopted mosaic to line the holiest parts of sanctuaries. The Cordova decorations, carried out under Caliph Al Hakim II between 961 and 968 involve only plants, but are vital for grasping the artistic scope of a civilization undergoing rapid change from late antiquity to medieval. Islamic art went on to make much use of multicoloured effects obtained by juxtaposing small ceramic tiles in various colours which were produced in large quantities and used for creating series of the same geometric motifs. It is another form of mosaic that abandons tesserae and takes up small components of various fundamental geometric shapes. As Islamic decoration became mainly geometric, this technique spread equally throughout the Mediterranean and even in Asia for several centuries.

The mosaics of the Adriatic area can be briefly summed up in an essay on the techniques and images used in the decoration of St Mark's in Venice. Probably this huge site incorporated mosaic work even in the eleventh century, but during the Middle Ages these were constantly altered, restored and replaced, so that little remains of the oldest wall decorations. Much influenced by Byzantine contacts, a school of mosaic developed out of Ravenna and Trieste from the late eleventh century onwards, to which the earliest decorations in

St Mark's belong. Artists, perhaps from Byzantium, but strongly influenced by local elements, recover a neoclassic Greek style. The mosaic of the ancient apse in the Basilica Ursiana in Ravenna, destroyed in the eighteenth century, though some fragments have been preserved, is dated 1112. The fairly intricate imagery shows how mature the artists had become in this tradition. To the same ambit belong the decoration of the two apses in modern Cappella di San Giusto in Trieste, providing further examples of mosaic development in the northern extremity of the Adriatic. In one of them, the Virgin, seated amongst archangels, holds up the Child; in the other, Christ standing is flanked by two saints.

The work of these artists, who made most of the mosaics in the region, makes use of cultural developments in the area marked by Ravenna and Venice, which were beholden to Byzantine and Eastern styles. This influence is clear in the old cathedral of Ferrara where at least the choir was adorned with mosaics, of which a head of the Virgin remains. In the lagoon of Venice, the apsidal mosaic in SS. Maria e Donato on Murano shows a solemn frontal picture of the Virgin standing, a design repeated in the apsidal conch in the Basilica of Torcello. The date of the Murano mosaic remains disputed but the fairly similar style of that in Torcello would indicate it is no earlier than 1150. In the early twelfth century, mosaics from workshops on the site of St Mark's, having absorbed various Byzantine currents, developed a truly Venetian style. Learning from much older illuminated manuscripts, such as the Cotton *Genesis*, a late fifth-century Alexandrian codex, and adopting what had entered the Venetian sphere from the West, artists prepared the way for a merging of Byzantine taste and the new Gothic style of Italy.

Since the Middle Ages, the basilica of St Mark's in Venice has been a true gallery of mosaic. The religious center of the Republic, it shows in its rich decoration the Doges' will to power and symbolizes the shift to the West of the artistic wealth of Constantinople. The intricate plan, which can be traced only in outline because of the constant refashioning of the mosaics, concentrates on the praise of Christ and the Universal Church, while also stressing the role of the church and politics of Venice. Decoration of the dome began in the late twelfth century. The oldest part, belonging to the first great plan, shows the young Christ in the center, surrounded by the Virgin and prophets, though the present mosaic dates from a thirteenth-century restoration. Comparison of these with Sicilian mosaics, and particularly those in Cefalù, shows analogies in style, especially in the Pentecost cupola. The cupola of the Ascension follows around the turn of the century, with an imposing Christ figure set in a mandorla surrounded by angels. Here we find the first genuinely Western traits between the windows: personifications of the Virtues and Beatitudes, and of the Four Rivers of Paradise placed under figures of the four evangelists. Under the cupola there are scenes of the Temptation, the Entry into Jerusalem, the Washing of Feet, the Last Supper, scenes from the Passion, and others. A little later came the cupola of St John the Evangelist, with scenes from his life on gold ground.

The pictorial schemes of the Basilica of St Mark continue on the southern transept with scenes from the life of the Virgin and of Christ's childhood, on the galleries with the story of St Mark, and in the central nave with the Sermon on the Mount. The date is about 1220, when the mosaics of the narthex and particularly the Genesis cupola were achieved. Indeed, decoration of the main façade began after the fall of Constantinople in 1204, as did construction and decoration of the great porch. The story of the Old Testament unfolds on the six cupolas starting with Genesis, followed by the life of Abraham, Joseph and Moses. It took over sixty years to decorate them, starting round 1200. The lunettes in the façade are to convey to the outside particular events such as the Translation of the Body of St Mark, over the left entrance.

Without doubt these mosaics influenced mosaic work in other areas of Italy. In 1218 Pope Honorius III sent a letter to the Doge Sebastian Zani to thank him for having sent an artist to Rome and asking for the loan of others to decorate the apse of San Paolo-fuori-le-Mura. It is also likely that Venetian artists helped in the rise of the Florentine school at that time. Its work began in 1225, with the first mosaics in the Baptistry of San Giovanni, with a noted part played by a Franciscan monk called Jacopo. Here we notice that artists had travelled, for the style is now Venetian, now Roman, and finishes as Florentine. Working through the whole of the thirteenth century, the mosaics of this Baptistry unfold a pictorial scheme that converges towards the center of the cupola adorned with plant and animal motifs, surrounded by the figures of heavenly spirits. The octagonal partition allows a narrative to proceed, interrupted only by the picture of the Last Judgement. We find scenes from Genesis, the story of Joseph, the Annunciation and the childhood of Christ, His ministry and Passion. Here for the first time arose the question of how the world of painting affected that of mosaic.

As the field of great Florentine painting developed, these mosaics constantly involved more and more famous artists and in particular Cimabue. His work in Florence seems to come after his time in Rome, where he had studied the craft with Pietro Cavallini. Along with other less famous artists such as Gaddo Gaddi, Cimabue took part in the work at the Baptistry in the late thirteenth century and added a new dimension to mosaic technique. Whether he had a hand in some parts of the story of Joseph remains debatable, but he is accepted as having contributed to the apsidal mosaic in the Cathedral of Pisa, as payment documents from 1301 and 1302 have indicated. This is the only documented work of Cimabue, who at Pisa succeeded a Master Francesco and was specifically commissioned to execute some pictures alongside the Christ. The Florentine group lasted into the late thirteenth century, with San Miniato al Monte and then at the Cathedral with the Coronation of the Virgin. In the latter, Gaddo Gaddi probably participated, a further link between Florence and Rome, since he also worked on the façade of Santa Maria Maggiore.

Round 1300, Italy saw great activity in wall mosaics, with many famous sites and artists. In 1291, Pietro Cavallini worked on seven panels adorning the triumphal arch and the apsidal walls in the Basilica of Santa Maria in Trastevere with scenes from Christ's childhood and the life of the Virgin. In surrounding and completing the mosaic at the back of the apse, executed over a century before, Cavallini's work symbolizes the continuity of the craft in Rome, in a neo-Hellenistic style with traces of Giotto. In San Giovanni in Laterano as in Santa Maria Maggiore, Jacopo Torriti, a contemporary of Cavallini, also revealed his art. Its full splendour stands out in the apse of Santa Maria Maggiore, with a signature revealing the nature of the craft: IACOB(US) TORRITI PICTOR H(OC) OP(US) MOSAIC(UM) FEC(IT). Like Cimabue and Cavallini, Torriti was a well known painter and worked in the upper church at Assisi, for example. In Santa Maria Maggiore the main theme is the Coronation of the Virgin, standing out on a ground decoration of acanthus foliage typical of the city of Rome. Under the apsidal bowl, either side of the Death of the Virgin are four episodes of Christ's infancy.

Beside the mosaics on the façade of Santa Maria Maggiore or in the chapel of the Sancta Sanctorum, we must mention those in Santa Maria in Aracoeli depicting the Virgin and Child between St John the Baptist and St Francis who present a Roman dignitary to them. Special mention must go to a mosaic modified in the seventeenth century which has enjoyed great acclaim because of its creator's reputation, and the role of the monument that housed it. The mosaic of the *Navicella* (Boat) was under the portico of St Peter's in the top part of the front wall at the main entrance. It shows Peter being saved by Jesus, picturing the boat with sails folded back and the apostles on board, probably started by Giotto in 1298. There has been much discussion as to the precise date of the work and its commission and to the exact role Giotto played in its execution. It is thought to date to between 1305 and 1310–1313. Some think Giotto's part was only an initial fresco then transformed into mosaic. Two fragments of the mosaic are extant: two busts of angels, one in the Vatican Grottoes and the other at Boville Ernica (south of Rome near Frosinone).

Looking at these panels in Giotto's style allows us to distinguish the master's work from that of his assistants, and to suggest a date of around 1300–1310. In Rome, as elsewhere in Italy, mosaic was used throughout the fourteenth century, in Pisa, Siena, Orvieto, in St Mark's in Venice, and the link between medieval Gothicism and early Italian Renaissance is clear. Moreover, being more lasting than wall painting, this technique was widely used on façades. Santa Maria Maggiore and Santa Maria in Trastevere are further proof of these ornamental façades that project the religious decoration of the church to public places. It is a tradition from late antiquity through the early Middle Ages, to which belongs the decoration of the Basilica of Parenzo in Istria, the Cathedral of Spoleto and San Frediano in Lucca.

Wall mosaic was almost exclusively Italian. Its reputation was so great during the Middle Ages that bishops and rulers went to great lengths to import this artistic form into their lands. The Cosmati, a Roman family of architects, sculptors and mosaic workers, travelled widely reaching as far afield as Westminster Abbey in England. Except for some documented examples, Romanesque and Gothic art produced no wall mosaics in the West. Abbot Suger, the great innovator of the pictorial schemes for the abbey church of St Denis, was much influenced by his trips to Italy. He chose to adorn one of the tympana in the western façade of the basilica with a mosaic, but his writings clearly state that this was going against the then current fashion in northern France. Examples in Prague are clear evidence of the export of Italian techniques and their degree of integration into northern artistic trends in the late fourteenth century. In spite of repeated attempts to adopt wall mosaic outside Italy, it remained exclusive to medieval Italian art. Only floor mosaics became widespread throughout the West during the Middle Ages.

Floor mosaic

In Rome as in Ravenna, in Venice and in northern Italy as a whole, certain pavements enable us to link the tradition of late antiquity with the new fashions of medieval Romanesque. At Terrassa in Catalonia one can see how techniques developed from the fourth to the tenth century. In south-western Gaul some rather later mosaics seem to give some at least visual continuity, with Romanesque mosaicists from Saint-Sever or Sorde-l'Abbaye from the late eleventh century copying plant decorations on ancient sites and merging them into Romanesque pavements. This imitation, or the weight of tradition, is seen in Italy too, for example in St Mark's in Venice or in Apulia.

Mosaicists used only local materials for their tesserae. In medieval times they often made use of only three colours, white, black and red. The re-use of old fragments of marble, porphyry or other hard stone was as common as working with tesserae from ancient mosaics. For example, in the mid nineteenth century, this practice was crucial to the restorers of mosaic floors in St Mark's in Venice. These artists had lists of Roman villas in the area that could supply tesserae or columns and other marble blocks from which to cut cubes. Mixing *opus sectile* with *opus tessellatum* techniques made the re-use of these materials easier. In San Donato on Murano, the large marble slabs in *opus tessellatum* are re-used pieces from sarcophagi or transoms of late antiquity. Cosmati floors in Rome use porphyry or marble disks that have been cut crosswise from columns. Such materials were even sent far away at enormous cost, from Rome to Monte Cassino or Sicily, for instance.

Medieval mosaics were produced by teams working from a preliminary sketch of the plan with the work split up into clear units. These can be identified in some floors by the join lines that correspond to the area covered by the tesserae on wooden frames used as a kind of casing for keeping the mortar fresh. Such techniques, well known from late antiquity and, for example, from the mosaics of Piazza Armerina, are observed in Romanesque mosaics in Otranto, Venice and Ganagobie. Various groups of craftsmen work together simultaneously on a plan traced out beforehand. Mosaic flooring is an expensive form of decoration and therefore is usually confined to an area round the altar of a church, sometimes extending to the choir and transept. In some exceptional cases such as those in Otranto, Venice or Rome, the mosaic covers the whole floor space like a huge unrolled carpet. Inscriptions at Otranto tell us about the time it took to lay such floors, suggesting that the work was slow, in this case taking over two years. The inscriptions are mainly sparing as regards personal details of patrons and artists. The person who ordered the execution of the floor is sometimes mentioned with the inscription *fieri iussit*, and is always a cleric: Archbishop Gionato in Otranto, Abbot Biagio at Santa Maria del Patir, Abbot Guglielmo at San Giovanni Evangelista in Ravenna, Bishop Gui in Lascar and Prior Bertrand in Ganagobie. In Otranto, beside the main inscription, another concerns the client, Gionata. There is a true link between the imagery and the client's personality. One particular inscription in Ganagobie acknowledges the roles of the client and the artist. The latter is generally not given so much recognition.

It has often been said that floor mosaic imitates the carpets that used to adorn churches and palaces. We know that the carpet of San Servatius of Quedlinburg has images very like those of floor mosaics. The arrangement of the mosaic panels often brings to mind floors covered with carpets in mosques. Though the structure of the decoration often resembles that on carpets, the designs are much more varied, often derived from distant sources familiar through trade in textiles and materials. The style of floors usually adapts itself to the art of the region where the building stands, particularly that of monumental sculpture and miniatures. Though style is conditioned by technical limitations, the floor images generally follow the evolution of the other arts of the time and run parallel to the imagery of mosaics on walls and vaults. On floors, images are meant to be discovered as one advances through the building, and often each of them relates to the part of the edifice which it adorns: altar, choir, intercolumnar space, passage and so on. Some themes are in principle excluded from floor mosaic such as Christ, the Virgin and in general scenes from the New Testament, since it would be irreverent to walk on them.

The content of floor mosaics generally belongs to particular iconographic series, above all the Old Testament, with particular recurring scenes or narrative cycles prefiguring the New Testament. Most floors favour Adam and Eve though the stories of Samson, Jonah or David feature a great deal. The lives of local saints figure largely in medieval floor mosaics, along with themes inspired by ancient mythology, literary cycles, popular legend or history, for example the rise of Alexander, the story of Constantinople, Arthurian legend and various episodes from the crusades. Another group of images even more common in floor mosaic concerns those involving cosmology, geography and maps. The personification of the twelve months, the twelve signs of the zodiac, pictures of the four seasons, the four cardinal points, the winds, planets, the year, the sun, moon and elements, all illustrate the cosmic and geographic notions of floor mosaics in the churches of both East and West. The final and probably most common set of images is that of real or fantastic animals made popular by medieval collections of animal tales or bestiaries. Inspired by the ancient *Physiologus*, these contained a description of each animal with name and features followed by a moral allegory concerning its behaviour. Many floors, similar to other medieval objects and pictures, show sets of animals shut in shelters and pens, groups of animals fighting or geographically related animals within larger pictures. These schemes usually vary from region to region, but generally, the images of medieval floor mosaic will relate to the area they occupy within a religious building. The mosaics that followed these themes belong mainly to the late eleventh century or the early twelfth. Before them, mosaics from 900–1050, like those of Aquileia, Pomposa, Cervignano del

Friuli, San Nicolò on the Lido of Venice or Reims Cathedral, involve interlaced ornamentation of subtle decorative or plant motifs, typical of early Romanesque, and only rarely include the theme of animals.

The floor of Monte Cassino, commissioned by Abbot Desiderius (1066–1071), has often been considered a milestone for the spread of floor decoration in Italy. However, perhaps its influence was less considering the amount of regional variation and evolution that took place. The floor of Monte Cassino, made of *opus sectile* and encrustations, with some animals in the decoration, is famous because of its Byzantine links, from where artists came to work in the famous abbey. Echoes of this mosaic are found above all in the surrounding area of Campania, in Caserta Vecchia and Sant'Agata dei Goti, and also in the region of Venice, throughout southern Italy and in Rome.

In Rome, contributions and traditions that made up the Romanesque mosaic are easier to identify. Some purely geometric floors from the early Middle Ages reveal that the art of mosaic had never been abandoned since late antiquity. Splendid examples can be found in Santa Maria Antiqua, San Crisogeno, San Clemente and the Quattro Santi Incoronati. A special style mosaic also developed for church furniture in Rome. The art and craft of Roman marble closely linked mosaic and sculpture, especially in the creation of Cosmati work by the brilliant Roman family of artists. In these highly coloured floors the decoration is almost wholly geometric, consisting of various alignments of large disks. The art evolved as it was passed from father to son. The Roman master Paolo decorated the transoms in the Cathedral of Ferentino (1108–1110). His four sons together signed the ciborium of San Lorenzo-fuori-le-Mura. More famous still were the Vassalletto family who, for at least a century after 1130, dominated the Roman market. They were responsible for the decorations in the cloisters of San Giovanni in Laterano, dated 1232 and 1236, and were obviously inspired as often happens by Cosmati marble work, both wall and floor.

In comparison, Sicilian floor mosaics bear witness to the Norman era in Palermo (La Martorana, the Cappella Palatina, San Cataldo, the Cathedral), in Monreale and other centers. The decorations do not always take up Roman features, but the use of large porphyry disks is noticeable. In Calabria, the floor mosaic of Sant'Adriano at San Demetrio Corona lies between the Roman-Campanian traditions and the Sicilian style. In Apulia, the floor of Santa Maria on the Tremiti islands, shows the start of figured Romanesque floor decoration around 1050. Animals and geometric motifs in *opus tessellatum* here reveal a continuity with late antiquity and the beginnings of large new figurative work. The floors of Pomposa, of around 1026, and of the great apse in the patriarchal basilica of Aquileia, about 1031, embody the same phenomenon in north-east Italy. During the second half of the twelfth century, the floors of Otranto, Trani, Taranto, Bari and Termoli formed a group typifying the great and varied illustration of Old Testament episodes, of scenes personifying the months and themes from literature and mythology. The floors of Otranto and Trani date to 1163–1165 and probably came from the same mosaic workshop. At the other end of the Adriatic, the Venetian lagoon produced a fairly uniform output of floor mosaics marked by alternation of *opus sectile* and *opus tessellatum*. They are adorned by geometric designs enriched with animal figures often from Western models, for example the story of the Burial of Renart which occurs so frequently. The floor mosaic of San Donato on Murano with an inscription dating it to 1141, allows us to date a group of works, of which the pavement of St Mark's in Venice is the most noted. Between Apulia and the Venetian lagoon, the floor of San Giovanni Evangelista in Ravenna adorned with scenes from the fourth crusade, or that of the Cathedral of Pesaro provide a stylistic link with central Italy. The splendour of pictorial schemes is probably greatest in southern Italy, to judge by extant examples.

Architectural decoration in black and white contrasts with the rich colour of large floors like that in Bobbio. Among the best, the Tuscan examples of Florence, Arezzo and Prato are a class by themselves. The two pavements in

San Savino in Piacenza one of which is in the crypt, the other in the raised choir, form large pictorial schemes similar to those in the ancient church of San Salvatore in Turin. To these synthetic monumental designs, which also pay great attention to detail, are added pavements where decoration is reduced to simple line illustrations, like that of miniatures in manuscripts of the time. Northern examples are the mosaics of Vercelli (in Museo Leone), of which an extant panel shows David and his musicians, as well as parts of warlike scenes. In the Cathedral of Casale Monferrato, and in the panel preserved in Ivrea which depicts the liberal arts, there are similar features. The pavement of the ancient abbey church of San Benedetto Po near Mantua is a case apart because of the huge scheme and its implicit historical and political bearing. The mosaic, inscribed 1151, is a high point of Romanesque art.

Not too far from Italian territory, in Haute Provence, the floor mosaic of Ganagobie adorns the transept and the three apses of a splendid church. It has become even more important since the recent discovery of another mosaic from the same workshop at Saint-André-de-Losans. Horsemen, monsters and various animals are comparable to those of the mosaics in Pavia. As far as Lyons, various fine floor mosaics have been preserved. At Saint-Paul-Trois-Châteaux (La Drôme) there is an unusual floor design centered on Ezekiel's vision. In the ancient episcopal chapel of Die, again from the second half of the twelfth century, a geographic and cosmographic scheme shows the winds, the Rivers of Paradise, and animals surrounding a circular image of the world, consisting of the celestial sphere, sun, moon and the stars. At Cruas, in the Ardèche, the prophets Elijah and Enoch are seen standing, under the hand of God. Southern French medieval floor mosaic extends to the south-west and to Catalonia. Amongst Catalan floors, the one that adorned the Basilica of Ripoll is perhaps the most famous. In front of the altar a carpet of circles decorated with animals accompanied a design of large dolphins. At Saint-Michel de Luxa a floor similar to that of Ripoll had been started, while large schemes of architectural sculpture were in progress. Except for a few fragments, these two floors have been lost. Five floors in south-west France form a fairly coherent group. The oldest, at Saint-Sever and Sorde-l'Abbaye, resume the plant and animal themes of ancient mosaics in the region. At Sorde, we note a gradual appearance of figurative decoration. In the early twelfth century, at Layrac and Moissac, appear the first pictorial subjects (Samson, the yearly cycle of work, the ascent of Alexander). About 1140 at Lescar, figurative decoration invades the floor in scenes of boar hunting and animal fights, for example.

Fewer French than Italian pavements survive, but the occasional mention and accidental discoveries have revealed the existence of floor mosaics in many important medieval Romanesque buildings in places such as Saint-Martin in Autun, Flavigny, Tournus, Vézelay, Cluny, Saint-Martin in Tours, Saint-Etienne in Nevers and the Cathedral of Orléans. In Lyons as in other large medieval cities, many religious buildings had mosaic floors. The oldest date to consecrations of the time when Pope Pascal II visited Lyons, when Gaucerand was bishop, in the early twelfth century. One of these two clerics was shown life-size in front of the altar of the church of Saint-Martin in Ainay. The latest mosaic in Lyons is actually the one with a richer and fuller pictorial scheme. In the church of Saint-Irénée the theme centered on the life of the martyr saint Irenaeus, with images of the liberal arts and the virtues. Reims, another great medieval city, had several floor mosaics. That in the monastic choir of Saint-Rémy, now destroyed, had an elaborate scheme featuring the figures of Jerome, the evangelists, apostles and prophets. With King David placed at the entrance, pictures of the earth, the sea, the four rivers of Paradise, the seasons and the liberal arts, were accompanied by those of the zodiac, the months, the virtues and the cardinal points. Beside the altar there were a series of scenes from the Old Testament in what could be seen to reveal the encyclopedic thought of the period.

While in southern France, mosaic floors can be compared directly with the monumental sculpture of the time, in the north the links seem closer to manuscripts and stained glass. In the abbey church of Saint-Denis the twelve months of the year encircled a kneeling monk at prayer. At Saint-Omer, in the abbey church of Saint-Bertin, the pictures of King David, the prophets and probably Solomon, were accompanied by the gravestone of William of Flanders, who died in 1109. The zodiacal signs encircled a design very similar in style to certain pictures in the *Liber floritus* produced in Saint-Bertin around 1120.

In England, beside the earlier cited Cosmati mosaics of Westminster Abbey, we must mention a twelfth-century pavement in Canterbury Cathedral, made of stone slabs encrusted with mastic and showing rich imagery. In technique, it is one of a group of decorated pavements, examples of which can be found in Hildesheim in Germany, Saint-Nicaise in Reims, and Wiślica in Poland. The latter mosaic, of about 1170, is one of the most northern examples to have survived. In the Rhineland, amongst figured *opus tessellatum* mosaics, that of the crypt in St Gereon in Cologne, completely restored, wholly concerns Old Testament episodes, particularly the cycles of David and Samson. The mosaic dates from 1151–1156, as does the tomb of Abbot Gilbert at Maria Laach. Everywhere, from northern Italy to the north of Europe, floor mosaics and the ambitious pictorial schemes were suddenly abandoned towards 1250. The rapid growth in the production of glazed ceramic tiles replaced the expensive craft of floor mosaic. Only a few isolated pavements, like those of the Baptistry in Florence or in the Cathedral of Siena, provide a clear link between Romanesque and Renaissance.

On page 177: floor fragment, Cathedral of Ivrea, now preserved in the Seminary. The mosaic piece (3.32 × 1.34 m [10½ × 4 ft]) is from the floor of the Romanesque cathedral and shows the Liberal Arts with inscriptions. This image is often shown on Romanesque floors and sometimes topped (witness Saint-Rémy in Reims) by a picture of Wisdom: from the fountain of Wisdom run the seven streams of the Liberal Arts of the Trivium and Quadrivium.

Below: detail of floor mosaic, Ganagobie, France. These mosaics adorn the three apses and the transept of the church and show the work of Provençal mosaicists and their link with northern Italy. Geometric carpets unfold alongside pictures of monsters and horsemen. Animal images from bestiaries complete the design. An inscription mentions the prior Bertrand and a certain master Pierre Trutbert, fixing the date after 1135. A mosaic from the same workshop was recently discovered in Saint-André in Rosans, Haute Provence.

Opposite: two details from mosaics in the Basilica of Otranto. The largest Romanesque floor mosaic extant in *opus tesselatum*, it has been restored several times. Two inscriptions indicate a date of c. 1163–1165, mentioning the artist Pantaleone and the client Gionata, archbishop of Otranto.

On pages 180–181: floor detail, abbey church of Pomposa. These mosaics are the first example in the north Adriatic area. Mixing *opus sectile* with *opus tesselatum* and using only a few animals as figures, this mosaic (c. 1026) and that in the patriarchal basilica of Aquileia shed light on the local continuity of plant decoration and help explain the subsequent flourishing of Venetian pavements.

Below: apsidal floor, old cathedral of Lescar. The latest mosaic in southwestern France has been identified by an inscription ascribing the pavement to the wish of Gui de Lescar (1115–1141). On wide bands surrounding the altar a set of scenes unfolds, with animals fighting, the strange picture of a dog or wolf attached to the tail of an ass, and episodes from the boar hunt. The style must be ignored, since there has been much nineteenth-century restoration.

Below: Asti Cathedral. Floor mosaic showing Samson fighting the lion. Twelfth century. Northern Italy had many mosaic pavements; a few notable examples are in the museums of Reggio Emilia and Pavia.

On pages 184–185: apse of San Clemente, Rome. The mosaic covers the apse and the triumphal arch of the upper church; it is a clear example of the revival of early Christianity in the early twelfth century. On the gold ground lie rich bunches of acanthus; a cross adorned with twelve doves, symbol of the apostles, resumes an old Christian theme. The novelty lies in the representation of the crucified Christ, who is unclothed and dead.

On pages 186–187: apse of Santa Maria in Trastevere, Rome. Decorated under Pope Innocent II between 1140 and 1143, or soon after. The Virgin alongside Christ on a huge throne is a new element, an intermediate stage going towards the crowning of the Virgin, found later in the apse of Santa Maria Maggiore. Here prominence is still given to Christ who protects the Virgin with his arm. The axial position of Christ copies earlier designs.

AGIOS
PAVLVS

DECRVCELAVRENTIPAVLO
FAMVLAREDOCENTIS

ISAIAS

GLORIA INEXCELSISDEOSEDENTISVPTHRONVM

IENT
NAMIN
ELEC IETHO
TANEA
NUM
ETPOMEUM

PETRVS

CORNELI YSPP

IVLIVS

LEPODIVS PBR

SISTITVR IN TEMPL

Below: apse of Cefalù Cathedral. Its mosaics date from c. 1148, according to the inscription. The majestic picture of Christ Pantocrator as a bust occupying the conch of the apse has severe features, the right hand blesses and the left holds a book. The image offers evidence of Byzantine designs being adopted in Sicily, via mosaicists who came from Byzantium in around 1140–50.

Below: Monreale, cathedral apse. A new Byzantine trend invades Sicily about 1180, under William II, and is seen at its strongest in this apse. Built on three levels, as in Cefalù Cathedral, it shows various pictures. The bust of Christ Pantocrator in the conch is modelled on Cefalù. A comparison of the two reveals the differences between the two almost coeval workshops of the same area.

Below: cupola in Santa Maria dell'Ammiraglio (La Martorana), Palermo. In spite of the changes made between 1500 and 1600, this small church preserves some mosaics that exhibit a marked merging with architecture. Made under Roger II, in the mid twelfth century, they stress the links between church and state in Norman Sicily.

Opposite: Cappella Palatina, Palermo. In the cupola, Christ Pantocrator is depicted as Lord of the Universe, above the Kings of the Earth: "the sky (Uranus) is my throne," the inscription says, "and the archangels are the guard."

Below: Royal Palace, Palermo. The mosaics in the chamber of King Roger have been partly preserved (known as King Roger's, though going back to William I [1154–1166]). Hunting scenes and animals standing face to face are seen on a gold ground rich in plasticity among gardens with many plants. The walls and ceiling show the influence of Roman villas of late antiquity and how the ostentation of Islamic art appealed to rulers.

Opposite: cupola of Santa Maria dell'Ammiraglo (La Martorana), Palermo. King Roger II receives the crown directly from Christ. There are clear links in ideology and style with Byzantine mosaic.

On page 194: Great Mosque, Damascus. On page 195: interior and detail of the Dome of the Rock, Jerusalem. The mosaics extant in the Great Mosque of Damascus, along with those of the residence of Khirbat al-Mafjar, the cupola of the Dome of the Rock and the Al-Aqsa Mosque, show how far the Eastern Umayyads adopted mosaic art. The decorations are reminiscent of Hellenistic and Alexandrian landscape elements, showing how the new rulers absorbed the art they found in the eastern Mediterranean.

ΡΟΓΕ ΡΙΟС ΡΗΞ   ΙС   ΧС

Below: Great Mosque, Cordova, the mihrab. These mosaics are a good example of Western wall mosaic in the tenth century. With only plant motifs rich in shape and colour, these huge mosaics decorate the privileged area of the mosque. They reveal various hints of the Byzantine mosaic of the eastern Mediterranean. The caliph Al Hakam II is said to have sent a delegation to Nicephorus II Phocas (963–969) in search of mosaic specialists.

Opposite: Great Mosque, Cordova, arch to the right of the mahrib. Completed in 965. The mosaics of this mosque are the peak of tenth-century non-figurative mosaic.

197

Opposite and below: San Giusto, Trieste. Apses with *Christ standing* between two saints and the *Virgin and Child*. In today's Cappella del Santo Sacramento (below), which was originally the main apse of the Basilica of Santa Maria Assunta, a large design devoted to the Virgin and Child unfolds on a golden ground. On the two sides, the archangels Michael and Gabriel stand erect, as do the apostles on the lower band. The mosaic has been variously dated from the eleventh to the twelfth century but when compared with St Mark's in Venice, early twelfth century seems the most likely date.

On pages 200–201: Santa Maria Assunta, Torcello. Detail of *Last Judgement*. This is perhaps the largest picture of its kind to have survived. In the upper part, Christ is represented crucified flanked by the Virgin and St John. The linking of the Crucifixion and Last Judgement suggests a widening of iconography towards the Second Coming. Begun in the late eleventh century, there were partial refacings a century later. Several phases of restoration date from the nineteenth century.

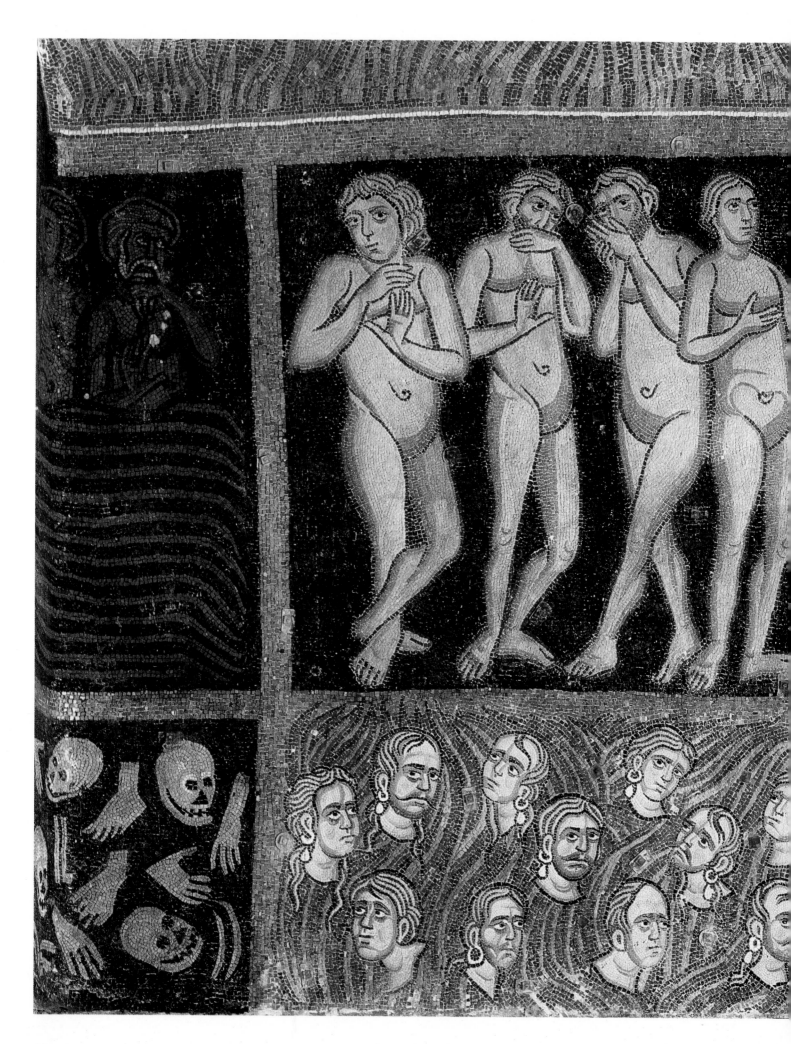

Opposite: St Mark's, Venice, *Christ on the Mount of Olives*. The picture dominates the central nave above figures of the prophets: it is one of the masterpieces of the basilica, dated c. 1220. The theme had already been represented in Venice, in a painting in San Nicolò del Lido (late eleventh century), but is a recurrent subject in Byzantine art, and already present in the Cathedral of Monreale. The mosaicists, perhaps three, who worked on this mosaic, gradually leave Byzantine models behind and converge in creating a new Venetian style.

Below: St Mark's, Venice. Mosaic with *Translation of the body of St Mark*. Found over a side door, this mosaic gives an accurate picture of the church in 1220: it has the four bronze horses brought from Constantinople in 1204 and on the main door a bust of the Redeemer in mosaic, instead of today's picture of St Mark by Lorenzo Lotto.

On pages 204–205: St Mark's, Venice. *Last Supper*, on the large vault between the central cupola and the left side of St Mark's; it goes back to the mosaic phase of the early twelfth century. In spite of the many Byzantine elements in the figures, the design has no depth and thus belongs to Romanesque art.

Left: St Mark's, Venice, narthex cupola of the *Creation*. This opens the vast series of *Genesis* mosaics in the narthex. Carried out probably around 1220, the decoration of this cupola is in three concentric circles adorned with separated bands of images. The narrative cycle is devoted to the phases of Creation, in distinct sectors. The images recall illuminated manuscripts and have links with an Alexandrian Bible of the fifth–sixth centuries, the Cotton Bible. The proportions of the figures and the style reveal the first contacts with Western medieval art.

Left: St Mark's, Venice, *The prophet Jeremiah*. In the central nave of St Mark's, mosaics reach an unequalled artistic peak, seen especially in the prophets on the north and south walls, at the sides of Christ and the Virgin (c. 1220).

Opposite: St Mark's, Venice. *The Kiss of Judas*. Among the scenes unfolding around the cupola, partly dedicated to the Passion, the episode of the Kiss of Judas is particularly intense. Dating from perhaps 1180–90, the scenes in the Ascension cupola were made by various groups of eastern mosaicists. Strongly influenced by illustrations in Byzantine manuscripts and eastern mosaics, the panel shows in linear profile alongside the immobile figure of Christ the many mid-Byzantine and western sources gathered in St Mark's around 1200.

CRV
CIFI
GAT
VR ·

Opposite: St John's Baptistry, Florence. This church is among the foremost Italian monuments, not least for its mosaics. Begun c. 1225, it took nearly eighty years to finish. A huge *Last Judgement* makes up the largest part with Old Testament scenes and the life of John the Baptist, separated by small columns forming the rest. Between Venice and Rome, it is here in this Baptistry that Florentine mosaicists matured, and great artists like Cimabue, primarily a painter, adapted themselves to the requirements of mosaic.

Below: apse, Cathedral of Pisa. *Christ in Majesty.* This is the only documented work by Cimabue. Christ occupies almost the entire apse, leaving little space for the side figures of Virgin and St John (it is the latter figure who is mentioned in a document of 1302 as the work of Cimabue). The apsidal composition was finished in 1321 by Vincino da Pistoia. The St John of Pisa is regarded as one of Cimabue's masterpieces.

Right: Florence Cathedral. The mosaic
represents a common Gothic theme: the
Coronation of the Virgin in a celestial
setting, in the tympanum over the
central internal door. It is an important
source of information on the art of
Gaddo Gaddi, well known in Florence in
the late thirteenth and early fourteenth
centuries for his work on the Baptistry.

213

Below and opposite: San Pietro Ispano, Boville Ernica; and (opposite) *Angels*, Vatican Grottoes, Rome. These two early fourteenth-century mosaics, each 65 cm (2 ft 2 in) in diameter, probably come from the frame of the famous *Navicella* mosaic that was under the portico of St Peter's in Rome, in the upper part of the wall at the front entrance. The episode shows Christ saving Peter, and the ship carrying the apostles. An inscription indicates that the Boville fragment, detached in 1610, was transported there in 1612. Comparision with the Vatican fragment confirms that Giotto and his students had a considerable hand in the work.

Below: Santa Maria in Trastevere, Rome. *Offering to the Virgin*, by Pietro Cavallini. Below the mosaic in the vault of the apse, some rectangular panels were made just before 1291 under the direction of Cavallini. The picture refers to scenes of the donation. Here the kneeling buyer, Bertoldo Stefaneschi, is presented by St Peter to the Virgin and Child enclosed in a medallion. Paul, on the other side of the panel balances the design. While Peter and Paul with their severe posture recall the Romanesque tradition, the kneeling figure of the donor introduces the first humanist elements.

Below: Santa Maria in Trastevere, Rome. *Dormition*, by Pietro Cavallini. While some stylistic traits recall wall painting and the final fusion of Romanesque and Byzantine styles, the choice of images reflects new strains in Gothic art. During the thirteenth century, scenes from the life of the Virgin, particularly the Dormition, are often shown on cathedral façades.

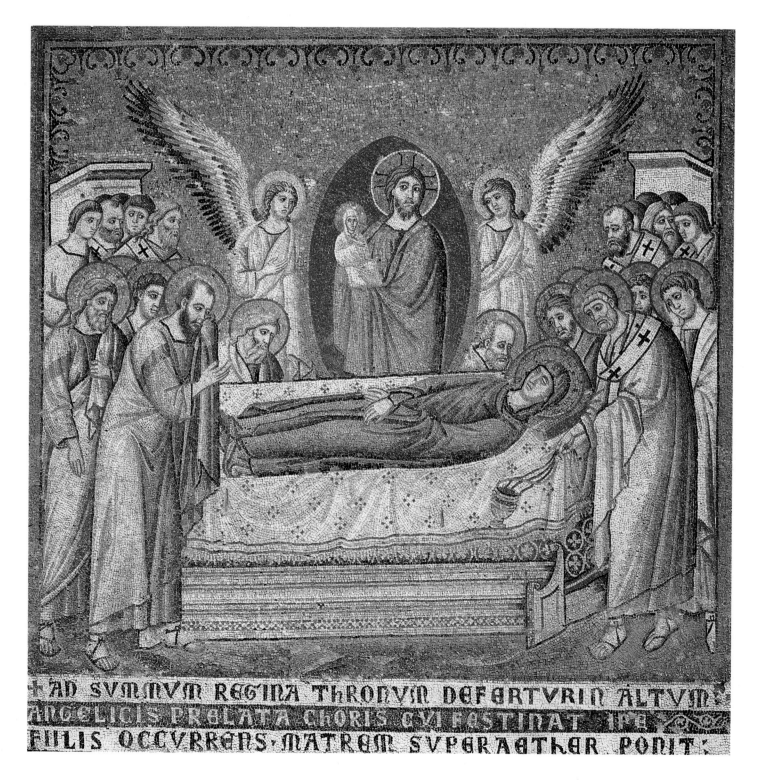

217

TABERNA   MERITORIA

IAM PVERVM·IAM SVNTE PATER
ACCIPIMVS·GENITVM TIBI QVEM DO

Left: Santa Maria in Trastevere, *Nativity*, by Pietro Cavallini. The episode continues the artist's cycle with all its stylistic novelties, and here in particular a great fidelity to Byzantine sources. The Virgin in a reclining position follows eastern tradition. On the right, there is a reference to the good tidings to the shepherds. The whole is set within a triangle. The inscription "Taberna meritoria" alludes to the legend of the ancient foundation of the church, said to be at a tavern on the right bank of the Tiber reserved for distinguished soldiers.

MARIA VIRGO ASSVPTA E AD ETHEREV ThALAMV IN QVO REX REGV STELLATO SEDE
EXALTATA EST SANCTA DEI GENITRIX SVPER CHOROS ANGELORVM AD CELESTIA REG

Left: Santa Maria Maggiore, Rome, main apse, mosaics by Jacopo Torriti. The scene is dedicated to the *Coronation of the Virgin*, with images principally from Gothic art. Compared with Santa Maria in Trastevere, over a century older, the theme has developed in the Gothic spirit of the late thirteenth century (1295). Jacopo Torriti, who also renovated the apse of San Giovanni in Laterano, here shows his way of welcoming the elements of an older tradition (for example, the acanthus leaves) and setting them beside newer stylistic and pictorial trends. On one side of the Coronation we see Peter, Paul, Francis and Pope Nicolas IV who commissioned the work; on the other, John the Baptist, James, Anthony and Cardinal Jacopo Colonna.

Opposite: Santa Maria Maggiore, Rome, façade mosaics, *The Patrician John before the Pope*. The panel of Christ on the façade is accompanied by four mosaics on the history of the basilica's foundation; ordered by the cardinals Jacopo and Pietro Colonna and carried out shortly after those in the apse, they are revealing as to life in Rome. At Christ's feet an inscription mentions the mosaicist Filippo Rusuti. In spite of the signature, it remains uncertain who made the subsidiary panels.

Below: Santa Maria Maggiore, Rome. Tomb of Gonsalvo Rodriguez, cardinal bishop of Albano and formerly archbishop of Toledo, died 1299. It is signed by master Giovanni Cosmos "civis romanus." Sculptor and architect, he here acts as mosaicist too, in typical Cosmatesque ornamentation, and in the setting here shown, with the cardinal kneeling before the Virgin and Child, flanked by Saints Matthew and Jerome holding scrolls showing where their relics are in the basilica.

On page 224: façade of Spoleto Cathedral. *Deeisis*. When Pope Innocent III consecrated the façade of Sant'Eufemia in 1198, it cannot have been complete, since its mosaic dates from 1207. The characteristic apsidal decoration of Christ enthroned between the Virgin and St John the Evangelist has been transferred to the façade. The work is signed by Doctor Solsternus who calls it an exercise "in modern art." In spite of restorations, for instance to St John's head, the mosaic bears witness to the merging of mosaic and architecture in central Italy.

RENAISSANCE MOSAICS

At the beginning of the fourteenth century the apse of Pisa Cathedral was completed and the mosaicists had finished their decoration of the dome of the Baptistry in Florence. In Venice work continued on the Baptistry and Sant'Isidoro's chapel in St Mark's whilst the century's largest mosaic project was probably the façade of Orvieto Cathedral. In one of Maitani's early design sketches, to which reference is made in a note of charges dated 1310, the intention seems to have been to cover the spire with mosaics. Documentary evidence of the work dates back to July 1345, when Giovanni di Bonino, who is now believed to be the great master of the Giotto school known as Maestro di Figline, was at work on the great window in the choir. The only surviving mosaic, *The Birth of the Virgin*, dates from 1365 and is now in the Victoria and Albert Museum, London, the others having been largely renewed during restoration. Originally this mosaic bore the signatures of Buccio Leonardelli and Ugolino di Prete Ilario. The year afterwards Brother Giovanni Leonardelli was to create the mosaic of the Assumption over the main door; a head from this work is now in the Opera del Duomo, the Cathedral Museum. Fourteenth-century Umbrian mosaics were conceived as large paintings expressed in mosaic. They are also identifiable by the use of large tesserae separated by wide interstices of cement, and by the artists' clear intention to achieve an illusion of volume.

It is surprising to find the same artistic notions in the mosaics on the façade of the Cathedral of St Vitus in Prague which Emperor Charles IV commissioned in 1370. Apart from Orvieto Cathedral, it is the only Gothic building in which a very large surface area is covered with mosaic, here depicting the Last Judgement. It has been suggested that this typically Mediterranean art form was brought to Prague by Venetian craftsmen. But neither the style nor the technique correspond with what we know of fourteenth-century Venetian mosaic. However, its tessellated acanthus clusters decorate piers which divide the façade in exactly the same way as those in the Reliquary of the Holy Corporal in the Cathedral of Orvieto and the pronounced classicism of the nudes in the Prague mosaic are very reminiscent of the contemporary Umbrian school of painting. The mosaic technique is also very similar to that used by the craftsmen in Orvieto. Orvieto owed much of its prestige to possession of the linen altar cloth where, in 1263, drops of blood appeared while a Bohemian priest was celebrating Mass in Bolsena. Charles IV would certainly have heard of the work in progress at Orvieto during his visit to Italy in 1368–9. It is therefore not unlikely that patterns and mosaicists were recruited there for Prague.

The mosaics in the Chapel of Sant'Isidoro in Venice were started after 1355. The Venetian craftsmen who created them were more faithful to the Romanesque tradition, as seen in *the Virtues* depicted in the central cupola, and less interested in the latest sophisticated refinements of Paleologus mosaic. Their fellow craftsmen, at work on the mosaics of St Mark's Baptistry during the same period, seem to have favoured a slightly different artistic approach by turning to the passing from old Byzantine tradition to the Gothic learnings of the schools of the Po Valley, typified by the works of the great contemporary painter, Paolo Veneziano.

Towards the end of that century the Tuscan painter Cennino Cennini, at that time in the service of the Carraresi in Padua, was compiling his *Libro dell'arte* (*The Craftsman's Handbook*). Despite the work in progress in St Mark's, this work reveals a total lack of knowledge of wall mosaic. To him "mosaics" mean the imitation Tuscan mosaics, painted in tempera on a base of shells and bits of feather, or stained and engraved glass. He had in mind the wall decoration using glass plaquettes which imitated the Cosmatesque mosaic style and was adopted so confidently by Andrea Orcagna in his work on the Or San Michele tabernacle. The situation became even more tragic when a fire ravaged the basilica of St Mark's in 1419 and there was no one in Venice capable of replacing the mosaics. The search widened to Genoa where the master mosaicist Jacobello della Chiesa was known to have gone. Although he had previously worked in St Mark's, he refused to undertake this task. We know that Lorenzo Ghiberti was in Venice in 1425 and a few months later, when he had returned to Florence, Paolo Uccello was busy in St Mark's. It is likely that his master, Ghiberti, had recommended him. However, given that a letter written in 1432 by the workers of Santa Maria del Fiore refers to him as *maestro di musaicho* and reveals that they are aware of his having created a large picture of St Peter on the front of the Venetian basilica (evidence of which survives in a painting by Gentile Bellini), it is puzzling that this young Florentine could have acquired such expertise in a decorative art of which his fellow Florentine Cennino Cennini was completely ignorant.

Evidence that a certain Giuliano Pesello was being paid during the years 1414–16 for mosaics laid in the Or San Michele tabernacle is questionable as such confusion prevailed in Florence between glass plaquette decoration and real mosaics. We do know, however, that the John the Baptist niche in the exterior of Or San Michele by Ghiberti, completed between 1414 and 1416, had a tympanum with "side view of a prophet in mosaic." In such a site, the area to be covered would seem too large and too exposed to the elements for a large expanse of glass to have been feasible, and therefore it is much more likely that this was a real mosaic. It may well be then that Ghiberti, who was fascinated by the art forms of antiquity, could have revived this art which had hitherto been lost to Renaissance Florence.

From what we can discern from Gentile Bellini's copy, Paolo Uccello's mosaic broke away from the Venetian-Byzantine tradition of fusion between mosaic decoration and architecture. The saint is shown as angular and gesticulating, with great importance being given to the book he is holding. Its edge is portrayed in perspective, creating a tension with its architectural setting, like the statues which were being placed in the exterior niches of Or San Michele during this period. Muraro attributes to Paolo Uccello the designs for certain decorative motifs in various parts of the basilica, which must have been damaged by the fire. They clearly betray the intention of introducing a studied perspective, another element which is obviously at variance with antiquity's conception of mosaics. Paolo Uccello was also responsible for designing paving stones with geometric and perspective intarsia work in marble, a technique which was alien to the Venetian tradition but had for centuries past been very popular in Tuscany.

Paolo Uccello left Venice just before the most important mosaic project of the Renaissance got under way: the decoration of the St Mark's Chapel of the Mascoli. By now the crisis caused by the lack of master mosaicists was over; thirty years later Filarete was to record that there were kilns in production in Murano which specialized in the production of tesserae for mosaic, although he does regret the fact that their quality is not "as good as it used to be in days gone by."

The chapel was at that time simply known as the "new" chapel and was only to acquire its present name in 1614. It had been built in 1430 at the behest of the Doge, Francesco Foscari, perhaps as an ex-voto expressing his gratitude to God for having survived an assassination attempt. In 1449 the scaffolding was still in place. The chapel included many new architectural features, such as the marble triptych on the altar, the architectonic arrangements reminiscent of Ghiberti's and Michelozzi's work and which incorporate niches containing statues sculpted by a Florentine master. The well-defined veining in the red jasper surrounding the triptych which seems to echo the form in ever widening ripples, is also a new departure from the Byzantine tradition which had hitherto held sway in St Mark's and which had required the marble flagstones to provide a subdued and tranquil ground below the wall mosaics. A scroll in the mosaics of the vault bears the signature *Michael çanbono venetus fecit*, but Michele Giambono was certainly not its sole artist and, indeed, scholars have discovered that Andrea del Castagno and Jacopo Bellini worked on them and also probably Lorenzo di Pietro, known as Il Vecchietta.

From the entrance to the far wall, along its entire length, the top of the barrel vault which covers the chapel is traversed by a gold fascia on which is a pattern of foliage and palmettes. Despite the floridly Gothic stylization, it bears a remarkably close resemblance to the illuminations and frontispieces of twelfth-century Byzantine manuscripts. The fascia is broken by three medallions, two containing busts of prophets and the center one the Virgin and Child. The idea of placing medallions with busts of the saints in the vault is clearly inspired by Giotto's paintings in the Chapel of the Scrovegni but it is worth mentioning that Giambono, who was certainly responsible for all three, had envisaged the medallion with the Virgin in perspective as an oculus opening onto a starry sky. The intrados of the oculus is in red gold, whereas the Virgin Mary's halo is of paler gold. Since work had to proceed downwards, starting at the highest point of the vault, Giambono must have been in charge from the outset. He must also have made the decision to treat the cornices around the various sections of mosaic as salient features amid the various architectural arrangements and not as a means of fusing them which would have been in the Byzantine tradition. This is particularly well demonstrated by the cornice which surrounds the open oculus in the lunette at the far end and which, together with a window to the left, lightens the chapel. The oculus balances the scene of the Annunciation. Giambono was certainly the artist responsible for Mary but the design of the angel has a solidity and bulk to it which is far more Tuscan in inspiration, reminiscent of the angels which in 1437 were set below the tomb of Beato Pacifico in Santa Maria Gloriosa dei Frari in Venice. This juxtaposition may prove helpful in calculating the dates of the mosaics. Despite the marked difference between the decoration of the right side and the left side of the vault, it is in fact very probable that what we see today stems from the same general preparatory work resulting from decisions taken before 1440, for which Giambono must take most of the credit. One has only to view the two halves of the vault together to realize that on the right there are two separate scenes, each having its own construction of perspective based on a separate vanishing point, while on the left there are two compositions placed so that the lines of perspective of both converge towards an ideal vertical axis sited on the vault's meridian line. Effectively, one side of the vault displays two experiments in the type of *perspectiva artificialis* originally invented by Brunelleschi, while the other uses a system of perspective that unifies two visual compositions, already adopted by Masolino da Panicale around 1431 in the Branda Castiglioni chapel of San Clemente in Rome.

The chapel therefore sheds light on the vexed question of perspective, hotly disputed in Padua and Rome at that time. Another young Tuscan artist was summoned to complete the Brunelleschi perspectives. There is considerable justification for believing that the choice fell on Lorenzo di Pietro known as Il Vecchietta. He was a young artist from Siena who had painted excellent central perspectives for Masolino in Castiglione Olona, a particularly difficult task since his canvas consisted of the concave sections of a vault. In Venice, as a test he was first required to draw perspectives on the walls of the room set aside as the mosaicists workshop, and there the visitor to St Mark's can still see them to this day. Il Vecchietta's designs can best be described as very unassuming: three triangular tympanums are repeated, with the center one recessed into the surface, and the lateral ones slightly projecting. But Il Vecchietta's touch is unmistakable in the five medallions, with plump, rosy putti nestling among the luxuriant decoration of foliage in grey stone enlivened by gilt highlights which the artist chose for the cornices.

The two settings in which Giambono housed the *Birth of the Virgin* and the *Presentation of Mary in the Temple* are rich in Renaissance features in spite of a predominantly Gothic appearance: triangular tympanums similar to those designed by Il Vecchietta, others mixtilinear, such as the marble ones on the chapel's altar, numerous rectangular openings, pateras (small shields) and shells. The dome of the church stands out distinctly in silver shaded in blue on a gold background. The narrative elements are articulated with convincing attention to detail and great delicacy. The *Presentation of Mary* is a reworking of the interpretation by Taddei Gaddi and of portrayals of the theme by the great

French illuminators and miniaturists, the Limbourg brothers, only a few years before.

When Il Vecchietta departed, the completion of the other half of the vault became a problem. In 1442 another young Tuscan artist, Andrea de Castagno, was in Venice and put his signature to the frescoes in San Tarasio that year. He was chosen to complete the Mascoli project. Lorenzo di Pietro's timid interpretation did not convince Andrea del Castagno. In place of the fragmentary arrangement chosen by his Sienese predecessor, he depicted the Virgin's catafalque in his scene entitled *Funerali* (*Death of the Virgin*), in front of an immense triumphal arch, through which a city can be seen. He retained Il Vecchietta's idea of medallions positioned in the frieze but made them monumental and Roman. As a concession to Venetian taste his arch ended in a stone balustrade as was the custom in that city, while from the Sant'Isidoro chapel he borrowed the idea of painstakingly reproducing the veins of the marble in the mosaic, emphasizing the dramatic rather than the purely decorative effect. Finally, the position of the keystone of the arch was marked by a stern Christ, more sculpted than painted, who was shown taking His mother's soul into His hands, the soul taking the form of a small statue. The recumbent body of the Virgin was positioned, with a strict observance of perspective, between four candelabra which marked out the space receding into the distance. Castagno also stayed long enough to see the two apostles on the far left reach completion.

However, this artist was to depart without seeing all his design sketches become reality. A Venetian team was put in charge of the work (the last invoice is dated 1451) and they completed Il Vecchietta's unfinished scene, reproducing Corinthian capitals on the pilasters from Castagno's examples, while using Giambono's design for the protagonists of the *Visitation*. When it came to the *Death of the Virgin*, one of the original design's candelabras was omitted, showing a lack of understanding of its vital role as a spatial marker. In fact, the Venetian workers gave more substance to the faces of the remaining apostles on the right hand side. Giambono inserted a scroll bearing the word *fecit* at the feet of the last four apostles which he was able to complete, indicating that he had now accomplished the task which had been entrusted to him some fifteen years earlier. The five apostles who subsequently joined them were to be portrayed by yet another new artist, Jacopo Bellini.

The St Theodore lunette over the sacristy door has also been attributed to Andrea del Castagno. The work actually dates from forty years after Castagno had finished but is an important indication of how considerable the Florentine artist's influence was on mosaic technique in Venice. It contributed to the new Renaissance code being established for mosaics. In 1439 another fire badly damaged the basilica and more restoration had to be undertaken. In order to reinforce the southern vault of the south transept, a new arch had to be built. This was covered in mosaics in 1458, as we learn from the signatures of the two master mosaicists responsible for them: Antonio, who has unjustifiably been identified with a certain Florentine, Antonio di Jacopo, and Silvestro. Antonio proved far more faithful to Andrea del Castagno's plans, even if the linear treatment of the pictures precludes any possibility of his having actually participated in the execution of any of Castagno's designs. Silvestro, however, is curiously and pleasingly archaic. The choice of a linear style was a way to complement the surviving medieval mosaics, and would have prevailed in the interpretation of both the mosaicists and the authors of the cartoons.

Of particular interest, in the central cupola, is the section representing Libya in which one of the faces was by a Lombard master who had been influenced by Bramante. The whole apse of the basilica was redecorated in a studiedly archaic style in 1506. The master mosaicist in charge was Petrus, known as "Piero de Zerzi dal musaico," who created the picture of St Mark on the south face dated 1482 and who had learnt his craft in the workshop of Silvestro. Pietrus' apse which encapsulates a twelfth-century design, marks a total change of direction for the mosaicists of St Mark's. His praying Virgin of 1509 on the arch between the San Clemente chapel and the presbytery obviously represents a step towards the new classicism of Giovanni Bellini, as Otto Domus has so perceptively pointed out.

What had happened was something new in Venetian painting. When Antonello da Messina created his triptych for Santa Maria Gloriosa dei Frari in 1487, he had demonstrated the great realistic effect of the inclusion of architectural arrangements in ecclesiastical pictures, following the example of van Eyck and Giovanni Bellini, and had greatly extended the potential of mosaic. At last a once far-fetched suggestion appeared to be practicable. The master mosaicist Vincenzo Bastiani, who used patterns from various master artists, worked to a design created by his brother Lazzaro, a faithful member of Bellini's school, for his *Christ and the Samaritan Woman at the Well* in St Mark's. From the 1520s onwards, gifted master mosaicists such as Zuccato, Bianchini, Bartolomeo Bozza and Lorenzo Ceccato were developing astonishingly skilful techniques in order to reproduce paintings by Titian, Il Salviati, Jacopo Tintoretto, and Jacopo Palma with the utmost accuracy and splendour.

According to a popular and probably well-founded belief, Titian is supposed to have suggested to the Office of the Procurator of St Mark's that he should replace all the old and "ugly" mosaics with new, modern ones. On 22 December 1566 an edict from the Procurator forbade replacement of the old mosaics except where this was unavoidable. The attempt to protect them, however, seems not to have been particularly effective since the ban was frequently reiterated. The enthusiasm which Venetian painters evinced for mosaic gave rise to a whole series of problems for Renaissance painting: the light relationship between the gold and colour; the conceptual relationship between reality and invention; respect for tradition and its observance.

In the Camera degli Sposi in Mantua, Mantegna painted the vaults with an imitation mosaic gold background and marble bas-relief work, following an ancient tradition which Donatello had successfully revived. Now, painters such as Mantegna and Ercole Roberti exploited the illusionistic effects of these techniques. In 1499, in an apse of the Cathedral of Parma, Cristoforo Caselli painted a vault in imitation gold mosaic as a ground for his grotesques. These fantastic decorations had only recently been developed after their discovery a few years before in the caves of the Golden House of Nero in Rome. The use of gold fake mosaic henceforth became more widespread. A Lombard artist adopted this technique in a lunette in Sant'Onofrio in Rome where also the apsidal bowl-shaped vault was covered in imitation mosaic by Baldassarre Peruzzi. This artist, barely twenty years old, arrived in Rome having worked with young mosaicists in the north of Italy, such as Cesare da Sesto. It was probably in these circles that he developed his interest in mosaic which he then shared with Raphael. In 1508 Raphael painted in imitation mosaic the Stanza della Segnatura in the Vatican following work already completed by Il Sodoma. Around about the same year Peruzzi was involved in the creation of the first true mosaics in Rome. These were in the underground chapel of Sant'Elena in the Church of Santa Croce in Gerusalemme. They were to replace the mosaics of a recently demolished votive chapel decorated in mosaics from Galla Placidia, Valentiniano III and Onoria. Peruzzi was probably there in time to see them, take in some of the motifs and images and, above all, to appreciate the new effects of relief, of light and of the deep greens and reds on a gold ground. The resulting mosaics were some of the most exceptional of the Renaissance, combining the refined elegance of the Florentine mosaic involving a subtle play of varying shapes with fifteenth-century grandeur, possibly an original way of evoking early Christian mosaics which brings to mind the name of Michelozzo. By 1510 the mosaics were finished.

In April 1520 Raphael died leaving the Chigi chapel in Santa Maria del Popolo incomplete, among various other works. This was a project in which he had intended all three arts of sculpture, painting and architecture to be united.

Sculpture held sway at lower levels found on the tombs, in bas-reliefs on the altar and statues in the niches. The altar-piece was to be coloured by applying oil paints directly on to stone panels; then came the tambour of the dome decorated with frescoes and stuccowork and finally the dome itself which was to be covered in mosaic. Raphael left one drawing, for the Eternal Father in the clerestory, the circular aperture in the center of the cupola. But doubtless the other mosaics must mirror his general plan, which envisaged God the Creator as the Mover of the stars. These mosaics were carried out by the Venetian mosaicist, Luigi Pace, under a contract of 31 May 1520, and this date shows that the drawings and perhaps the cartoons for all the compositions must already have been prepared.

The mosaic dome of Santa Costanza is often cited as being a precursor and inspiration for Raphael, even though there is no iconographic link between them, nor do the separate frames in which Raphael's mosaics are set repeat the blending of scenes and grotesques which must have been breathtaking in the fourth-century edifice. As we have seen, the circular section set in the center of the dome imitates a real opening, like the one in the Pantheon, although in Santa Maria del Popolo there is no likelihood of glimpsing birds in flight in order to read the omens. In Raphael's false opening we see only God the Father. This architectural fiction proclaims its own unreality and expresses the strange sense of a mystical vision inspired by art. It must be remembered, however, that mosaic is not painting but a translation of painting, rather like wall tapestries. It is a painting in glass and stone and its plasticity is exploited to put the finishing touches to a monument in which the unity of the three arts proclaims the unity of life and celebrates the ability of the soul to merge with its own Creator.

So Venice exported its master mosaicists to Rome. To see examples of their artistry and delicacy one has only to stand in the great basilica of their native city and look about, for example, at the mosaic of St Geminiano and the head of a female saint, in the atrium of St Mark's, dating from 1535, by Francesco Zuccato after a cartoon of Titian's. *The Judgement of Solomon*, 1583, by Vincenzo Bianchini, thought to be after a cartoon by Sansovino, is a marvel of originality: a great golden archway sets the scene, the luminosity of the precious metal vying with the blue sky; various figures are positioned against the great gold archway, revealing its ambiguous spatial function. The glass fragments positioned at various angles do not reflect the long, slow beams of medieval mosaics but short, intense flashes of cold light. But the changes needed in St Mark's to achieve the eloquence of Counter-Reformation Mannerism did not always take such subtle forms. A direction profoundly alien to medieval mosaic decoration dictated the work, and was aided by the presence of the opening in the atrium through which one can see the archway with the *Last Judgement* inside the basilica. As part of the scheme, at the main entrance, an image of St Mark was executed by Lorenzo Lotto (1545) which probably took the place of an earlier image of the Pantocrator. Although the sixteenth-century mosaicists had in most places superseded former iconographic plans, there are many interesting echoes of the medieval world, as in the great *Tree of Jesse*, the creation of Giuseppe Salviati (1542–51), which Arcimboldi was to take as his model in Monza Cathedral.

It was not, however, in Venice that Renaissance mosaic reached the final stages of its splendour but in Rome, in St Peter's. In the Vatican basilica where Giotto's mosaic had always been admired throughout the Renaissance as an unquestioned masterpiece, mosaic was to reaffirm its continuity in history. It was realized in a bold way with an immense Greek and Latin inscription in mosaic, black letters on a gold background going round the entire church. This innovation is reminiscent of the Churches of SS. Sergius and Bacchus in Constantinople and San Bernardino in Urbino but unlike any other Roman church where inscriptions are usually limited to interior surfaces and to the apse. Mosaics occur in most parts of St Peter's, especially in the dome which is covered in them. In fact, in terms of area, this mosaic project constitutes the largest ever undertaken. The guidebooks always make a point of stressing the amazing scale of the mosaics in St Peter's: for example, in the pendentives of the dome, the pen which St Mark is holding is alone one and a half meters high. Decorative mosaic art developed differently in Florence where it was regarded as a sophisticated speciality set apart from the mainstream of decorative art. It was, quoted Vasari, *"La vera pittura per l'eternità"* (the true way of painting for eternity) attributing this opinion to Domenico del Ghirlandaio who in 1491 created the *Annunciation* with his brother David for the tympanum of the Porta della Mandorla in Santa Maria del Fiore achieving what is truly painting expressed in mosaic. Another of Andrea del Castagno's fellow artists, Alessandro Baldovinetti, who had also learnt his art from Domenico Veneziano, realized what problems of expression were inherent in mosaic. While following in the Vasari tradition, he was eager to learn this mysterious art and is said to have approached a visiting German itinerant mosaicist from whom "he learned all there was to know about the craft." There is probably only some truth in this story. Baldovinetti's mosaic on the arch over the Porta del Paradiso in the Baptistry of Florence shows he has actually followed instructions which Andrea del Castagno had given his Venetian mosaicists. There is a distinctive contrast between areas of light and shade and the treatment of large surface areas is less indicative of a German influence than of an apprenticeship served in Florence. Be that as it may, the angels which support the medallion containing a head of Christ are clearly echoes of mosaics in the San Zenone chapel in Santa Prassede, Rome. The pilgrim bound for Rome, mentioned by Vasari in the *Lives*, would have returned home with sketches made on the spot of the mosaics which enhanced its great buildings. Vasari also tells us that when Baldovinetti died, a chest in his house was found to contain "designs and sketches as well as a notebook on how to make mosaic cubes, the plaster and the method of work."

In Florence mosaic remained a rare speciality and Baldovinetti was, in fact, in charge of the workshop of the Baptistry as late as 1487, 1489, 1490 and 1491, "there being no one else who knew how things should be done." Thus it came to be the refined art of the miniaturist as it had been in the fourteenth century when copies were made of the Byzantine portative mosaics. Gherardo di Monte del Fiora, the great miniaturist, had his picture of Saint Zenobius displayed on the silver altar of the Baptistry, while Lorenzo de' Medici collected "small Greek mosaic tablets" and in 1500 Gherardo was praised in verse for having been the first to teach the Tuscans how to create pictures out of glass. Something of his miniaturist's elegance is perhaps discernible in Peruzzi's mosaics for Santa Croce in Gerusalemme.

As mosaic was set to become a rarefied and intriguing specialization, an imitation of reality and painting combined, Florentine Mannerism and all its new notions had only to draw on the possibilities of such a definition and use the technique to achieve the transformations. While almost returning to the ancient origins of Roman nymphaea decorated with shell and tessera mosaics, the grottoes of the Boboli Gardens were filled with stalactites, shells and mosaics in a subtle play of variations.

Some frescoes by Lelio Orsi (in the Galleria Estense, Modena) show how, in the Renaissance, people were acquainted with Roman mosaic floors with a white background, and how this extraordinary provincial painter was able to capture their imaginative charm. But Vasari was also aware of a more widespread type of mosaic which the Romans used for floors, laid out in black and white. Between the Renaissance and Baroque eras this type of mosaic was highly prized in Liguria. These were not mosaics made out of tesserae but of pebbles, similar to ones still found in Rhodes and other Greek islands. This type of mosaic found its way into villas in Lombardy from Lake Maggiore to those fanciful grottoes at Pirro Visconti Borromeo's villa in Lainate, Lombardy. They are elaborate coverings of imitation "hangings" made from pebbles, often coloured or painted, full of monsters and little cupids and were designed by Camillo Procaccini, as Alessandro Morandotti has recently discovered.

Below: façade of Orvieto Cathedral, the greatest mosaic site in Italy in the late fourteenth century. Today most of these mosaics have been extensively restored. The *Birth of Mary*, today in the Victoria and Albert Museum, London, comes from the triangular tympanum over the right portal. It bore the signatures of Giovanni Leonardelli and Ugolino di Prete Ilario with the year 1365. It was detached in 1785–1787 by the Romans Tomberli and Cerasoli and, after various adventures, arrived at the Victoria and Albert Museum in 1891. It had been restored several times, among others by Davide Ghirlandaio in 1492.

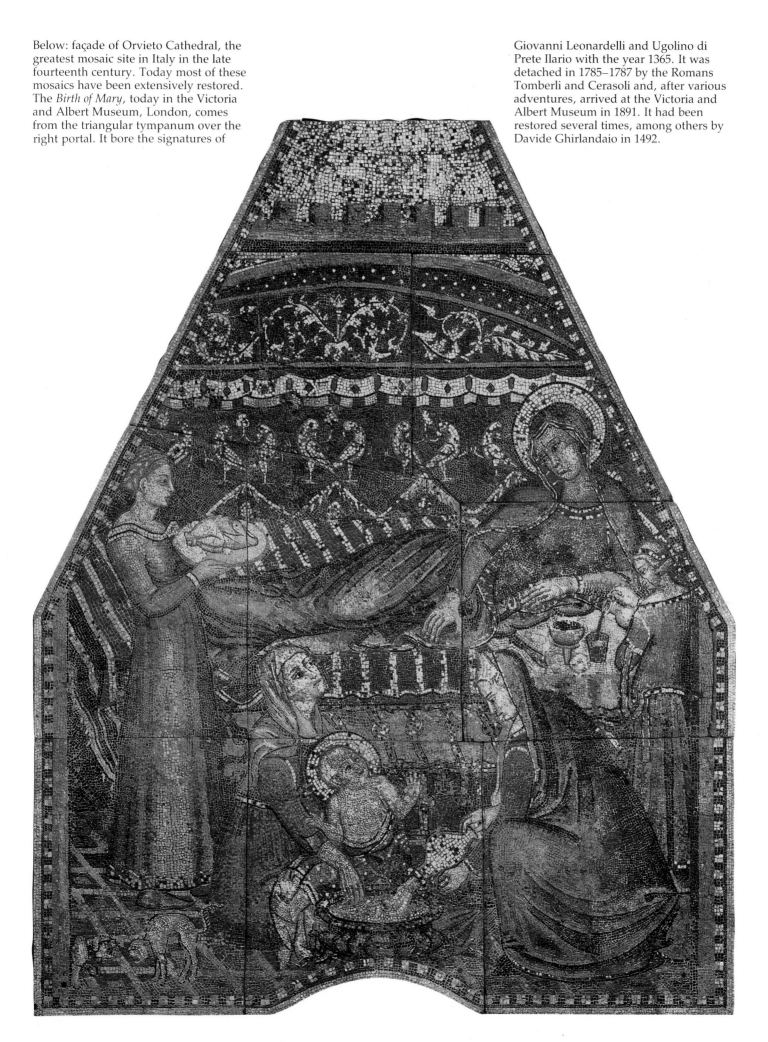

233

ECCE
ANG

AVE GRA
PLENA

234

On pages 234–235: Pisa Cathedral, *Annunciation*. In the late thirteenth century the mosaic plan for this church, which reached its height with Cimabue's collaboration on the mosaic in the main apse, was completed with the apses at the ends of the transept, with the *Assumption* to the right by a master close to Lippo Vanni of Siena, and an *Annunciation* to the left by a Pisan who sets Sienese motifs in severe, refined elegance.

Right: the transept façade of St Vitus Cathedral in Prague is a unique monumental mosaic north of the Alps. It is a valuable example of the Renaissance furthered by Emperor Charles IV of the House of Luxembourg who commissioned it and figures in it with his wife in the triangles near the central arch. The great golden triptych shows the *Last Judgement*. Italian artists certainly worked on it. The acanthus branches that adorn the buttresses are in Italian style and are found in the reliquary by Ugolino di Vieri of Siena in Orvieto Cathedral (1337–1338).

Below, opposite and on pages 240–241: St Mark's, Venice, Mascoli chapel. The only chapel built by a doge, the powerful and ambitious Francesco Foscari. Venetian and Tuscan artists took about ten years from 1432 to decorate it creating a great meeting point for the two figurative styles. There is only one signature, that of Michele Giambono, who completed the panel across the vault and directed the work from the start. However, the general design of the *Visitation* (opposite) and the execution as far as the decorative band under the three triangular tympanums is due to a Tuscan master, thought here to be Lorenzo di Pietro, or Il Vecchietta, from Siena. The *Death of the Virgin* (pages 240–241) is from a cartoon by Andrea Mantegna, but Venetian masters were responsible for the group of apostles on the right.

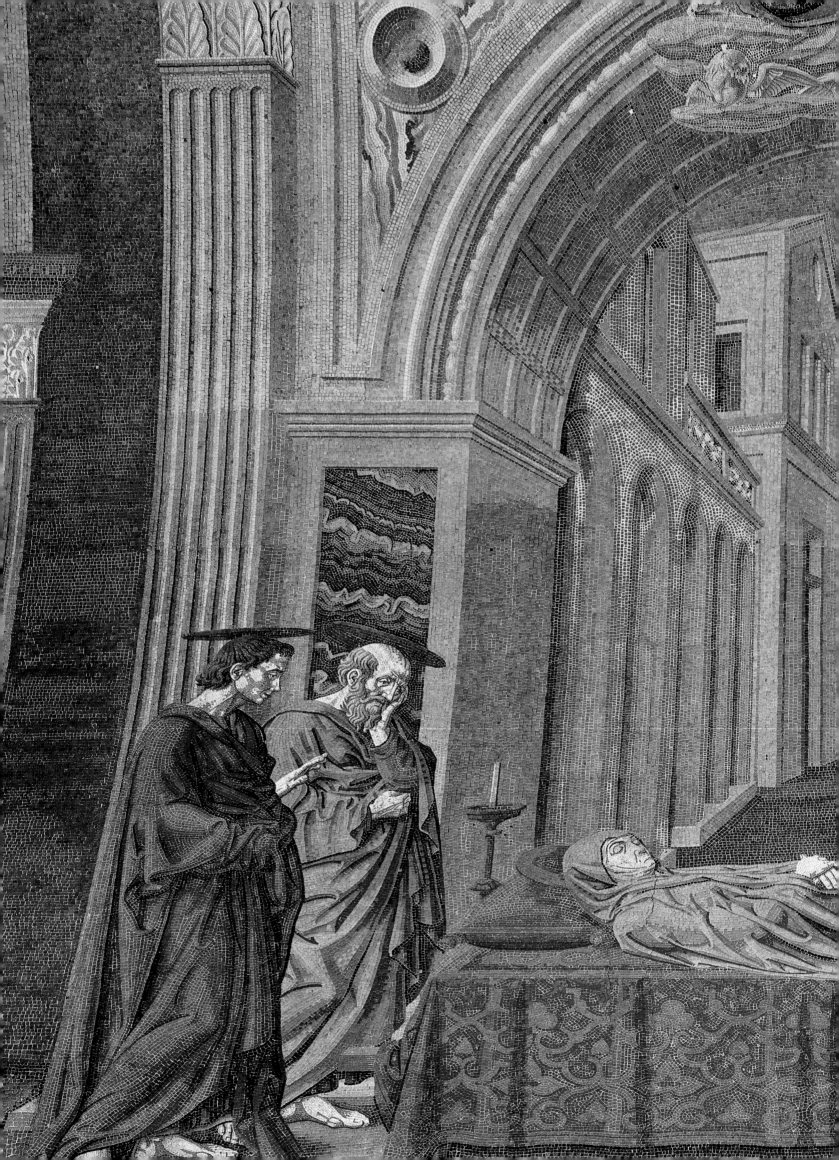

243

On pages 242–243: the small church of San Teodoro is part of the complex of St Mark's, Venice. In the lunette of the portal (late fifteenth century) a mosaic of St Theodore and the Dragon has been inserted from the destroyed church of Santa Maria Nova. The work is attributed to Mantegna, but also in part to Lazzaro Bastiani. The linear treatment of the hair recalls the mosaics of Silvestro who signed a figure in St Mark's in 1458.

Below: Florence Cathedral. The *Annunciation* by the brothers Domenico and Davide Ghirlandaio completed, in 1491, the scheme of the Mandorla door on the north side. The decoration of the door was begun by the last of the Florentine Gothic sculptors. It is of this mosaic, which took over a century, that Vasari has Domenico Ghirlandaio say "la vera pittura per l'eternità essere il mosaico" (true painting for eternity is mosaic).

Opposite: Opera del Duomo museum, Florence, mosaic with the bust of St Zenobius. Executed by Monte di Giovanni di Miniato, commissioned by contract in 1491 with the Ghirlandaio brothers and Sandro Botticelli to carry out mosaic decoration of the cathedral's Sacramento chapel.

Below and opposite: Basilica of Santa Croce in Gerusalemme, Rome. The underground chapel of Sant'Elena (opposite) replaced an earlier votive chapel with fifth-century mosaics. The author of the early sixteenth-century mosaics was probably Baldassare Peruzzi. He used complex Renaissance designs, but freely reused early Christian motifs. The bust of Christ (detail, below) at the top of the vault recalls the image of Christ Pantocrator in the cupolas of Byzantine churches.

Left: St Mark's, Venice, *Judgement of Solomon*. Starting with the refacing of the main apse by Silvestro in 1506, the mosaics of St Mark's were extensively renovated in the Renaissance. The *Judgement of Solomon* in the atrium was done by Vincenzo Bianchini in 1538. Vasari regarded it as "so beautiful that you could really do no better with the aid of paint." The cartoon has been attributed to Jacopo Sansovini, who in 1540 made the designs for mosaics by the Zuccato brothers, but the name of Giuseppe della Porta, known as Il Salviati, has been suggested.

Below: St Mark's, Venice. *Apocalypse.*
This mosaic, dating from 1570, was the
last by Francesco Zuccato, who had
begun work at the church in October
1524. Ten years later a mosaic by Zuccato
was sent to Emanuele Filiberto, Duke of
Savoy, who had hoped to employ
Venetian mosaicists at Turin. Vasari
notes that the scenes of the *Apocalypse*
are "so well made that looking at them
from below they seem to be painted in
oil with brushes." They were partly
destroyed and then restored in 1870 to
new cartoons by the *Società* of Salviati,
who had undertaken the restoration of
St Mark's mosaics. Francesco's brother
Valerio also helped with these mosaics.

Opposite: St Mark's, Venice. The mosaic
above the main portal was to show the
Saviour. In 1545, St Mark himself was
substituted, to a cartoon by Lorenzo
Lotto. The Lord's hand appearing
through the clouds refers to the original
scheme.

Left and below: St Peter's, Rome. The mosaics of the cupola are the largest ever made and mark the peak of the sixteenth-century style. The spherical vault, divided into sixteen ribs with six orders of mosaic was designed by Giuseppe Cesari, known as Cavaliere d'Arpino. The figures of the Evangelists are after a design by Cesare Nebbia (*Matthew* and *Mark*) and Giovanni de Vecchi (*Luke* and *John*).

254

Opposite: Boboli Gardens, Florence. Buontalenti grotto and fountain. The grotto was designed by Bernardo Buontalenti and built by him in 1583–1588 with the help of Giorgio Vasari and Baccio Bandinelli, in a true contest between art and nature. Apart from the statues, stalactites, imaginary landscapes and mosaics in pebbles and shells, they splendidly show natural matter dominated by intellectual form.

Below: Lainate, Lombardy. After 1587, the Bolognese painter Camillo Procaccini was charged with the decoration of the villa of Pirro Visconti Borromeo in Lainate, outside Milan on the Saronno road. In the park's grottoes the painter reveals infinite imagination in pebble mosaics on walls and some floors. On walls and vaults the natural colours of stones were often highlighted with paint.

On page 256: though renovated in the eighteenth and nineteenth centuries, these floor mosaics at Portofino represent a long and continuous Mediterranean tradition that was revived in the late Renaissance garden architecture of Genoa.

MOSAIC IN THE EIGHTEENTH CENTURY

In the eighteenth century mosaic technique greatly developed and spread as it was a time when ways of making new types of glass were found. These vital advancements helped to achieve projects begun in the seventeenth century but not always successfully completed, and to establish the art of miniature, detailed mosaic. It was mainly in the eighteenth century that St Peter's acquired its mosaic decoration, so that the mosaic art of this time is generally linked with the artistic and cultural life of Rome. Rome became the foremost producer of mosaics and the main center from which they spread, while artists developed specialized skills whose radius of influence extended beyond the Vatican, to the great cities of Italy and Europe and, in the early nineteenth century, even to America. The fashion had started in Rome, but came to involve the whole Western world and for a time set uniform standards.

There are three main uses of mosaic in the eighteenth century: first, to cover walls, an architectural art going back to antiquity; second, ample use in the miniature, portative fields; and finally, a new creative use in the goldsmith's art and in furnishing. The production comes from the Vatican mosaic Studio, a true industry set up in 1727 and still active today. It would be an important source of later innovation and inspiration. Unique in Europe, this Studio, from the end of Gregory XIII's pontificate (1572–1585) had as its main task to cover the interior of St Peter's with mosaic. The magnificent enterprise, which consciously aimed at rediscovering the spirit of early Christian decoration, offered great scope for artistic development. A school arose where an art a thousand years old could be handed directly from master to pupil while united in a working atmosphere where art and craft became manifest in daily stages. The presence of a stable body of mosaicists bound to one site was rare in that period and it constituted a source of expert artists for those requiring work in the field elsewhere.

In this way Venice, though foremost in making glass tesserae and rich in tradition as regards mosaic decoration, had no able mosaicists around the middle of the century. An expert on the seventeenth century, Pierre Saccardo, wrote that during the terrible plague of 1630 more than 46,000 people died in Venice and among these the most important mosaicists. By 1715 it had not yet been possible to assemble a new school, so that the work planned for St Mark's was entrusted to a Roman artist, Leopoldo da Pozzo, who then worked there till his death in 1745. His most significant mosaic is in the lunette of the second arch from the left in the façade, where we see the *Venetian magistrates revering the body of St Mark*. In central Italy, Orvieto with its magnificent cathedral is another seat where Roman mosaicists were at work. Among them was one of the most valued masters in the Vatican group, Filippo Cocchi the Elder, founder of a line of artists active in the St Peter's workshop far into the 1800s. In 1713–14 he executed the mosaic in the main spire of the cathedral façade of the *Coronation of the Virgin* after a copy by the Orvieto painter Ludovico Mazzanti from the original by Lanfranco.

From 1580, when a hard stone workshop was set up there, Florence had developed a center for producing furnishings, vases, tables and such items, gradually establishing production in *opus sectile* of precious or semi-precious stones such as jasper, quartz and chalcedony. In the eighteenth century, the output from this workshop greatly attracted the attention of visitors and thus prevented the city from working in the field of glass tesserae mosaic, in which Rome was so involved. In southern Italy, the situation was similar. Documents attest the presence in Palermo of Mattia Moretti, a mosaicist from the Vatican studio who, in 1753, was commissioned by Charles of Bourbon to restore the mosaics in the chapel of the royal palace. As a result, Moretti settled there and set up a school active mainly in restoring mosaics, directing it till his death in 1779. The school, based at the royal palace, lived on into the nineteenth century. Rome, in its role as training school for mosaicists, as reference point for all mosaic projects elsewhere, as a successful research center for new types of glass, was therefore a lively workshop for production and invention. Filippo Cocchi and Mattia Moretti, both active in the Vatican, developed and refined their technical experience in the delicate progress of the St Peter's mosaics, but at the same time they mark the end of a period and the start of a new one. Cocchi was the last artist of the first, truly heroic phase of decoration in St Peter's, while Moretti was part of a new, and in many ways very modern, order adopted by the Vatican studio from 1730. Both styles followed the principle, established by Vasari, that the aim of mosaic was to imitate painting, obtaining effects that deceive the eye and hiding the fine mesh that in the old technique highlighted each stage of the process. Imitating painting meant being equipped with tesserae of a wide range of colours just as a brush might easily create countless shades of any one colour. In the sixteenth and seventeenth centuries, to compare the results of a painter with those of a mosaicist could only work at a distance. In the eighteenth century it became a feasible exercise, to the delight of the artist and the viewer. This goal was reached thanks to some basic discoveries in the composition of glassy substances that go to form the body of the mosaic. It was work carried out in Rome under the auspices of the St Peter's workshop, whose task it was to look after all the operations and restoration work in the basilica.

Mosaic decoration began in St Peter's in 1576–8 and work lasted well on into the second half of the eighteenth century. This lapse of time can be seen in the difference in luminosity and texture between the cupola mosaics and the altar mosaics. The wall mosaics, except for some eighteenth-century parts, were the first to be made under the direction of famous artists, such as Girolamo Muziano and Paolo Rossetti, the pioneers of the enterprise, and during the seventeenth century Marcello Provenzale, Giovanni Battista Calandra, Guido Ubaldo Abbatini and Fabio Cristofari. Alongside these masters of mosaic technique and also painting, other artists supplied cartoons or supervised the work, men like Cristoforo Roncalli (known as Il Pomarancio), Giuseppe Cesari (known as the Cavaliere d'Arpino) and Pietro da Cortona. In this first phase, glass was imported from Venice where almost a monopoly on production was held. Venetian glass tesserae were brilliant and transparent in a way that produced different hues in the underlying colour depending on lighting conditions. In St Peter's, the mosaics in the six oval cupolas of the side aisles, in the main cupola, and in the four minor corner ones, do in fact diffuse a sparkle of coloured light that gives body to the subjects represented. However, this effect frustrated the aim of achieving the chromatic depth of painting and so, from 1600, the workshop tried to find glass compounds more suited to this task. They developed special furnaces and hoped that by increasing production they could reduce the Venetian monopoly. Soon after 1650, Rome was able to produce its own glass tesserae.

The second phase of Vatican mosaic covers the whole of the eighteenth century, in particular the mosaic reproduction of paintings above the altars of the basilica and the start of the production of various objects with sacred and secular subjects for private clients or otherwise reserved as gifts to high-ranking state visitors. This rested on two facts: the workshop nominating Pietro Paolo Cristofari as director and head of all painters active in St Peter's (19 July 1727) and the discovery at around about the same time of the great Roman glassworker Alessio Mattioli. He discovered, among other things, a way of producing opaque glass in a wide range of colours, a new type of metallic calcite-based paste which he called *scorzetta*, and purple, a colour much valued for its vividness, produced in sixty-eight hues. With Cristofari, the Vatican mosaic Studio became an established institution, rising to the level of an industry and developing a true spirit of enterprise. Mattioli's success in making glass tesserae removed any barriers preventing mosaics being any less than paintings. The new opaque cubes overcame the problem of the colour changing according to the light and, along with the various new tints, meant excellent results were achieved in the production of mosaics conceived as oil paintings to be seen from near-by. In 1731 the workshop gave Mattioli sole rights for supplying purple tesserae and the "complexion" tesserae needed for areas of flesh in figures.

As to the Studio's seventeenth-century output, foremost came the former project of making mosaic copies of the masterpieces in St Peter's, in order to allow the storage of the paintings in more suitable and securer places while leaving the decoration of altars unaltered in the form of fine mosaics. By 1711, only six mosaic panels had been completed: *The Archangel Michael* designed by Calandra from a cartoon by the Cavaliere d'Arpino (1628–30), not much favoured because the Venetian tesserae used were too brilliant and transparent, thus disturbing the overall scene; and five subjects begun by Fabio Cristofari: *St Nicholas* in the Crocifisso Chapel, near the Pietà, and the four placed at the base of the cupola pillars in the Grottoes, showing *St Longinus*, *St Helen*, *St Andrew* and *St Veronica* (from originals by Andrea Sacchi). Since 1709, Filippo Cocchi had been working on the picture of the *Martyrdom of Saints Processus and Martinian* from the original by Valentin. However, the transformation into mosaic of altarpieces in St Peter's really began with the *St Peter on Lake Tiberias* (known as the *Navicella*) by Pietro Paolo Cristofari (1720–1726). Having set up a stable group of mosaicists paid regularly from an agreed sum for the whole, Cristofari began reproducing the paintings as mosaics, a task that was to take decades, not only for St Peter's but also for Sicily, Portugal and (between 1788 and 1793) the Casa di Loreto. All the altarpieces now in St Peter's are eighteenth-century, except the *Deposition* from a Caravaggio original and the *Doubting Thomas* from one by Camuccini which are early nineteenth century.

When Cristofari was at the height of his work as director, the Studio was visited by Charles de Brosses, councillor and later president for life of the Parliament of Burgundy, who set down his impressions, printed later in *Lettres familières ecrites d'Italie en 1739 et 1740*. Distinguishing between small and large mosaics, he prefers the latter, especially if they lack the final finish, which was imparted to polish the surface but often made it too brilliant. Having observed that the main virtue of mosaic was that it preserves lively colours through time, he favours the idea of calling Roman mosaicists to France to decorate some galleries in Versailles with the frescoes of Raphael which adorn the *Stanze Vaticane*, and the splendid ceilings with those of the *Story of Psyche* in Villa Farnesina on Via della Lungara, Rome. This decision of de Brosses confirms that, as a center of mosaic art, Rome was unique, although it also begs the question of how the expertise of the masters was defined. Since it was a matter of reproducing paintings from cartoons by others, de Brosses thought of them as simple workmen, like those who made the Gobelins tapestries, since they had no notions of design and merely copied originals, scaled up or down or to size. This somewhat low estimation is contradicted by documents in the workshop's archives. For example, a note from the first half of the eighteenth century lists some of the artists in the Studio's first real group, defining them as "mosaic painters" (Giuseppe Ottaviani, Mattia Moretti, Guglielmo Palat, Bernardino Regoli, Enrico Enuo, Alessandro Cocchi, Nicola Onofri, Francesco Fiani) and ends by saying that Cocchi and Onofri are good painters, for "their work shows good taste and colour." Since the definition "mosaic painters" covers the whole group, presumably the other members too had some basic grasp of design and colour. Besides, towards the second half of the eighteenth century the Vatican school was subject to a strict rule: anyone admitted had to undergo an apprenticeship of up to four years under the guidance of experienced artists, and this may well have included instruction in drawing. Eighteenth-century mosaic altarpieces in St Peter's show no weakness in the colouring of their design. The series produced under Cristofari's supervision includes *Presentation of Mary at the Temple* by Francesco Romanelli, *Burial of St Petronilla* by Guercino, *Communion of St Jerome* by Domenichino, *Baptism of Christ* by C. Maratta, *St Peter baptizing the Centurion Cornelius* by A. Procaccini, *Martyrdom of St Sebastian* by Domenichino, *Martyrdom of SS. Processus and Martinian* by Valentin, begun by Cocchi in 1709, *St Wenceslas King of Bohemia* by A. Caroselli, and *Martyrdom of St Erasmus* by Poussin. Between 1744 and 1785 work continued with the addition of *The Immaculate Conception* by Pietro

Bianchi, *Mass of St Basil* by Subleyras, *St Peter healing the Cripple* by F. Mancini, *The Archangel Michael* by Guido Reni (to replace the earlier one by Calandra which was given to the Cathedral of Macerata where it has remained), *St Peter raising Tabitha* by Placido Costanzi, *Transfiguration* by Raphael, *The Miracle of St Gregory* by Andrea Sacchi, *Crucifixion of St Peter* by Reni and *Ecstasy of St Francis* by Domenichino.

At the beginning of the eighteenth century some wall decorations in certain cupolas were still incomplete, and the one in the Cappella del Battesimo had not been started. The planning was given to Francesco Trevisani in 1709. He made cartoons in stages from 1710 to 1745. The pictorial scheme alludes to salvation through baptism, by means of images from the Old and New Testaments. From 1710 to 1757 various parts were completed: the vault of the Cappella della Presentazione, after earlier cartoons by Maratta, with the *Glory of the Virgin*; the lunettes and vault of the Cappella del Coro, from cartoons by Marcantonio Franceschini and Niccolò Ricciolini, completing those left unfinished by Ciro Ferri, with biblical figures and the *Eternal One in Glory*; the lunettes and vault of the Cappella di San Michele, the earlier ones on cartoons by Bonaventura Lamberti (*Elijah* and *Tobias*) and by Marco Benefial (*St Peter baptizing St Petronilla* and *St Nicodemus giving communion to St Petronilla*), the latter with angels from cartoons by Ricciolini; the cupola of the Cappella della Madonna (or Cappella della Colonna) with devices alluding to the *Virgin* by Giuseppe Zoboli. Between 1768 and 1779 there was a re-working of the mosaics in the cupola of the Cappella Gregoriana, where decoration in St Peter's had begun, from cartoons by Salvatore Monosilio for the vault (*Attributes of the Virgin*) and on cartoons by Nicola La Piccola for the pendentives (*Doctors of the Church*). Under Cristofari's direction, the Studio devoted part of its efforts to private clients or to works for other places. Many were created for this purpose, among them two given to Maria Amalia of Saxony on her marriage to Charles of Bourbon, King of Naples. They were *The Saviour* by Reni and *The Virgin* by Maratta and are thought to be those now in the Palace of Aranjuez. Three made by Mattia Moretti in 1746–51 for the King of Portugal, showing *The Holy Spirit*, the *Annunciation* and the *Baptist* are presently untraceable. Of the same origin are the memorial portraits of *Maria Clementina Sobieski*, wife of James Edward Stuart in St Peter's, of *Cardinal Renato Imperiali* in the Roman church of Sant'Agostino, of *Cardinal Innico Caracciolo* in the Cathedral of Aversa and the double portrait of *Clement XII with his nephew Cardinal Neri Maria Corsini* in Palazzo Corsini in Rome. Amongst the secular subjects we are aware of two *Muses* from originals by Pietro Bianchi and exported by Philip V.

From 1700, along with a demand for mosaics and for artists willing to work outside the Papal State, foreign powers decided to set up their own production centers on the Vatican model. In the years 1739–40, the Elector of Saxony, on visiting Italy, tried to do so but failed. In Russia, with Empress Elizabeth Petrovna favouring an influx of European culture, a furnace and mosaic workshop were set up in St Petersburg in 1752. This was organized by the poet, scientist and mosaicist Mikhail Lomonosov, who carried out various works, among them the empress' portrait and the *Battle of Poltava* celebrating the glorious victory of Peter the Great. A mosaic portrait of the Tsarina Elizabeth Petrovna was done by the Roman Alessandro Cocchi and is now in the Hermitage in Leningrad along with many other mosaics by Lomonosov and others. When Lomonosov died in 1765, the eighteenth-century Russian workshop ceased to be. Only later in the nineteenth century, would there be a revival.

In the early 1870s, when the Vatican Studio went through a critical time, Rome saw the first steps of a new kind of mosaic using thread-like glass. The invention is generally attributed to Giacomo Raffaelli, a highly regarded and skilful mosaic painter of the eighteenth century. This new procedure arose from one type of Mattioli's glass. If reheated in a flame it became malleable and could be drawn out. This allowed one to extract long thin rods known as *filati*, an excellent matrix for the minutest tesserae, of even 1 mm across. The material lent itself to the most imaginative ideas and the Roman artists produced mosaic creations of hitherto unknown gracefulness and elegance.

In 1775 in his studio in Rome Giacomo Raffaelli presented the first exhibition of ornaments using these minute tesserae. In the same period other artists too had experimented with the technique, for example Cesare Aguatti who created the mosaic candelabra in the Salone degli Imperatori at Villa Borghese in the years 1784–85. There is a highly detailed mosaic of *Sybil's Temple* by Aguatti at Tivoli from 1774, indicating that even then there were products using minute tesserae. However, it was Raffaelli's exhibition that brought the new technique to the notice of a wider public.

In Rome, alongside the mosaics of large tesserae with cubes cut from a cake of glass placed on an iron blade on a block and then struck with a small hammer, there arose mosaics of small tesserae using the *filato* glass. The two types were linked by the common aim of achieving a painterly effect. The small mosaics at first went for designs using parallel rows of small square tesserae with a principal subject standing out from a uniform ground, clearly aiming to recall the features of older mosaics. Neoclassical culture was then at its height, and no doubt lay at the root of both ordered design and the themes represented. At the end of the eighteenth century and until 1810, there was a clear change in taste as artists tried to conceal divisions in the design structure by using either a colour range rich in tones or tesserae no longer bound to a square framework. This tendency was furthered by later refinements in technique such as that attributed to Antonio Aguatti, famous master of the small mosaic, who made *filati* in which several tones of the same colour were mixed providing various possible shades. These tesserae were highly useful for producing the subtlest transitions of light and colour.

From the start, miniature, detailed mosaic was applied to small objects for personal use, such as snuffboxes, perfume flasks and jewels, or to furnishings, such as paperweights, vases and household goods in general. In ornamental work, the most notable ideas concerned the decoration of table tops, cabinets, walled furniture and fireplaces. One of the first known to use mosaic for furniture was Pompeo Savini who in 1787 made a table top for Stanislaw Augustus of Poland. The choice of pictorial themes always rests on ancient or contemporary painting, but the small mosaic artist constantly captures subjects in this new medium with their full poetic force. At first it was the ancient material that provided inspiration, in particular the representation of details from everyday life found during excavations in Herculaneum and Pompeii and made widely known by the eight volumes of *Antichità di Ercolano Esposte*, published from 1757 to 1902. There are small domestic animals at play or sometimes even performing human activities, objects such as tripods, caskets, altars, amphoras and delicate female figures between flowing coloured veils, all part of the symbolic representation of human relations. An often repeated theme is that of the *Doves on the rim of a cup*, subject of a mosaic of the first century A.D. found in Hadrian's Villa at Tivoli in 1737, now in the Capitoline Museum in Rome. It was mentioned by Pliny the Elder in his *Historia Naturalis* and consequently the group became known as *Pliny's Doves*. However, this enthusiasm for classical and mythological themes was also accompanied by an interest in the current tastes of a society which was changing and entering a romantic phase. In the new cultural climate, landscape, vistas with ruins, animals resting or fighting, baskets or vases with flowers, genre scenes and popular costumes come to the fore.

Inspiration for the most frequent and best loved scenario is of course provided by the city of Rome and its countryside. The ruins of the Forums, the remains of the Colosseum and the Pantheon, but also the main Christian buildings with St Peter's foremost, are all constantly found to adorn ornamental surfaces of small objects and table tops where they created a symmetrical pattern of panoramic representations in various shapes and sizes. A wide public, mainly of lay and religious aristocrats, foreign travellers, diplomats and rulers on official visits, was at once conquered by these elegant creations and ensured their success, both artistic and commercial. The great circulation of travellers in Rome in the second half of the eighteenth century and thereafter ensured the spread of products in minute tesserae, often small enough for a few to be carried by one person to the main cities of Europe, the beginning of a profitable export trade that brought much revenue to Rome. Twenty years after Raffaelli's exhibition, miniature mosaic was already so great that in 1795 the Vatican workshop decided to make them in the Studio so as to be able to compete with private Roman workshops which had meanwhile sprung up in great number on the main tourist thoroughfares.

Again, the new impulse in mosaic technique in Rome inspired other countries to set up their own workshops on the model of that of St Peter's. In 1792 the French diplomat Hugo de Bassville wrote that it would be well to train at least three of the young men chosen to finish their studies in Rome in the art of mosaic, not only to allow France to conserve in mosaic copies the most famous works, but also to ensure to the country a part of the enormous sums that these crafts brought to Rome. He quoted the large sum of money paid for a copy of the *Doves* in France. In 1798 a Roman artist, Francesco Belloni, was asked to open a mosaic atelier in Paris. The capable young man went there and managed a successful center of production till 1832. England, too, set up a mosaic school at the South Kensington Museum, but it did not remain active for long. In Italy, the first city to set up an establishment on the Vatican model was Milan. Founded under the auspices of Prince Eugène de Beauharnais in 1803, it was directed by Giacomo Raffaelli from 1804. His best known work from this institute was Leonardo's *Last Supper* (now in the Church of the Minorites, Vienna). Naples had an active mosaic center from 1811 to 1814 run by Giovanni Battista Luchini, but it was only provisional. In 1824 Ferdinand IV appointed the Roman, Francesco De Poletti, to organize a permanent school on the Roman model, but the plan failed when the king died.

What the eighteenth-century public liked most in mosaic art was that it was more durable than painting and its colours retained their vividness. Hence the liking for large mosaics in cut glass tesserae, used to reproduce master paintings of all periods and considered more difficult to realize than small mosaic. Today we look at this differently, acknowledging the difficult balance between interpretation and imitation in any work, large or small, and allowing for the lengthy amount of time required for the process. Nevertheless, it must be said that small mosaic, besides being expressive and achieving splendid results, has helped to spread neoclassical and, later, romantic figurative themes because of the wide use made in the decoration of personal and domestic effects.

Below: *Scene with owl and other birds*, by Marcello Provenzale (1575–1639), Rome, 1616, 61 × 41 cm (2 ft × 1 ft 4 in). Argenti Museum, Pitti Palace, Florence, once the property of Cardinal Scipione Borghese. The presence in the background of the Fontana Paola, constructed in 1612 on the Janiculum hill in Rome for Paul V, uncle of the cardinal, makes it a family celebration of that pope's generosity. With great realism Provenzale catches the deep gaze of the owl who sits immobile on an oak branch, indifferent to the coming and going of the other small birds. The monochrome landscape, in delicate shades of grey, contrasts with the bright green leaves in the foreground, and the most varied hues of brown, yellow and red in the plumage of the birds.

On page 266: *St Peter on Lake Tiberias* (after a work by Lanfranco), by Pietro Paolo Cristofari (1685–1743) in Rome, 1720–1726. Mosaic in large cut tesserae. St Peter's, Rome. The painter Niccolò Ricciolini made the cartoon and Cristofari the mosaic. The work, lasting over six years, revealed the mosaicist's artistry and was a measure of the progress in Rome in the field of mosaic tesserae: the vast range of hues allowed chiaroscuro transitions equal to those in painting.

On page 267: *Transfiguration of Christ* (after a work by Raphael). Rome, 1759–1767. Mosaic in large cut tesserae. St Peter's, Rome. This mosaic copy of Raphael's famous painting, now in the Vatican Picture Gallery, was made after a cartoon by Salvatore Monosilio by the mosaicists G. F. Fiani, G. Palat, A. Cocchi, B. Regoli, P. Polverelli and V. Castellini. It demonstrates the great scale of hues which were available in the Vatican studio in the second half of the eighteenth century.

Below: *Maria Clementina Sobieski*, portrait by Pietro Paolo Cristofari (1685–1743). Rome, 1740–1742. Mosaic in cut tesserae. St Peter's, Rome. The funeral monument of the wife of James Edward Stuart (the Old Pretender), designed by the architect Filippo Barigioni, included sculptures by Pietro Bracci and the mosaic oval by Cristofari. The cartoon for the mosaic was by Ludovico Stern from the oil portrait now in the Scottish National Portrait Gallery, Edinburgh.

Opposite: *Persian Sybil* (from a work by Guido Reni), by Mattia Moretti (c. 1710–1779) in Rome 1737. Mosaic in cut tesserae, Uffizi Gallery, Florence. Commissioned by the Corsini family as a gift to the Grand Duke Peter Leopold of Tuscany on his visit to Rome; afterwards it was enriched by a frame in gilded wood bearing his coat of arms. It is after a painting now in the Gemäldegalerie, Vienna and has been attributed by some to Guido Reni. The mosaic is of great value for its fine workmanship, elegant shape and bright colours.

Below: *Cardinal Renato Imperiale*, portrait by Cristofari (1685–1743). Rome, after 1737. Mosaic in cut tesserae. Sant'Agostino, Rome. It is part of a funeral monument in the church. The plan is due to the architect Paolo Posi, the sculptures are by Pietro Bracci and the mosaic by Cristofari. The monument shares many features with the Maria Clementina Sobieski monument in St Peter's and shows the spread of the mosaicist's work beyond the Vatican.

Opposite: *Clement XII with his nephew Cardinal Neri Maria Corsini*, portrait by Cristofari (1685–1743). Rome 1730–1740. Mosaic in cut tesserae, 228 × 152 cm (7 ft 7 in × 5 ft ¾ in). Palazzo Corsini on Via della Lungara, Rome. From a portrait by the painter Agostino Masucci. Clement XII with his camauro, cassock, surplice and cape, sits on a throne and directs his thoughtful glance to the outside; the young cardinal stands on his right in his imposing robes of office.

Below: *The Muse Euterpe*, Filippo Cocchi (1740/50–1818). Rome 1785, signed and dated. Mosaic in cut tesserae, 90.5 × 100 cm (3 × 3¼ ft). Kunstindustrimuseum, Copenhagen. The mosaic is typical of Vatican studio productions as papal gifts to rulers and high officials. This one was given by Pius VI, whose coat of arms is part of the gilded bronze frame, to Princess Sophia Albertina of Sweden in 1793. Copied from the work by Raphael, the Muse is playing a lyre of seven strings while casting a rapturous glance towards the sky. Although there are doubts about the source and title, the mosaic is nevertheless of high quality, particularly in its smooth design and delicate modelling.

Below: *Three Dancing Hours*, by Pompeo Savini da Urbino (active in Rome in the second half of the eighteenth century), Rome 1766–1769. Mosaic in relief. Kunsthistorisches Museum, Vienna. After rediscovering the traditional art of relief mosaic, Savini applied it, under Cardinal Alessandro Albani's commission, to make a partial and small-scale copy of the bas-relief with the *Dancing Hours* formerly in the entrance of the Galleria Borghese and now in the Musée du Louvre, Paris. The mosaic signed by the artist was given by Cardinal Albani to Emperor Joseph II in 1769. The design seeks to relate the architectural division of the ground and the three dancers. While a fluid rhythm rules the steps of the two right hand figures, the left figure is somewhat cold and flat, as if worked by another technique.

Below: *View of Rome from the Janiculum hill*. Rome c. 1800; 51.1 × 134.3 cm (1 ft 8 in × 4 ft 5 in). Los Angeles County Museum of Art, donated by Mr and Mrs Gilbert. With few changes, the mosaic is derived from an etching of Giuseppe Vasi of 1765 entitled *Prospect of the noble city of Rome from the Janiculum hill*. The level at which the view is taken in line with the Palazzo Corsini gives a solemn and amplified picture of the city, ending on the horizon with a range of hills. The dense press of houses is a vivid document of urban growth in eighteenth-century Rome.

Below: *Plaque with symbolic motifs*, by
Giacomo Raffaelli (1753–1836). Rome
1792, signed and dated on back.
Miniature mosaic; 7 × 5.2 cm (2¾ × 2
in). Private collection, Rome. Neoclassic
taste appears in the fixed uniform white
ground on which a lyre, an olive branch
and three butterflies lie, but the airy link
between plane and objects removes the
sacred import sought by so many similar
pictures, creating a more fresh real-life
representation. The symbols refer mildly
and light-heartedly to the poetic virtues
of love.

Left: *Plaque with goldfinch*, by Giacomo Raffaelli (1753–1836). Rome 1798, signed and dated on back. Miniature mosaic; diameter 6.7 cm (2¾ in). Private collection, Rome. The uniform white ground and the outer band with recurrent chain motif, typical in miniature mosaic of 1780–1800, are neoclassic in character.

Right: *Plaque with tripod and other elements*, by Giacomo Raffaelli. Rome 1801, signed and dated. Miniature mosaic; diameter 6.2 cm (2½ in). Private collection, Rome. It is an example of the great ability of the artist who also carried out the famous reproduction of *The Last Supper* by Leonardo da Vinci (after a cartoon by Giuseppe Bossi) for the Minorite Church in Vienna.

Below: *Plaque with view of Flavian Amphitheater* (now the Colosseum), by Luigi Mascelli (c. 1770–1825). Rome, early nineteenth century. Red glass and gold miniature mosaic; 5.4 × 3.4 cm (2¼ × 1¼ in). L. Moroni Collection, Rome. The composition is typical of the period. Along with regular square tesserae to define the area, there are particles of glass in filament, circular, oval or rectangular shape to give body to the shaded effects of landscape, trees and wall work.

Opposite above: *Plaque with Pliny's Doves*. Rome, early nineteenth century, miniature mosaic; 7 × 4.7 cm (2¾ × 2 in). Private collection, Rome. The doves quenching their thirst from a cantharus is a favourite image in small mosaic, loved by both artists and public. It refers confidently to antiquity, resuming a subject of a mosaic picture excavated in Hadrian's Villa at Tivoli in 1737 and placed in the Capitoline Museums (1764) where it remains to be seen just as described by Pliny in *Naturalis Historia* (Book XXXV, chapter X).

Opposite below: *Plaque with parrot driving two turtles*. Rome, early nineteenth century. Miniature mosaic; 7.2 × 4.5 cm (2¾ × 1¾ in). Private collection, Rome. Again, antiquity supplies themes to resume and develop, particularly from paintings at Herculaneum. The use of a black ground leads to the mosaics of Gioacchino Barberi (1783–1857) who was among the first to devote himself to miniature mosaic and to have invented black glass tesserae on which he put the figurines in imitation of the paintings of Herculaneum.

Below: *Snuffbox with view of the Roman Forum*. Rome 1810–1820. Tortoise-shell, gold, miniature mosaic; 7.3 × 4.7 cm (3 × 2 in). L. Moroni Collection, Rome. The representation of the Roman Forum in miniature mosaic shows the area of excavation soon after the French government began work in 1810. It offers an original view from the foot of the Capitoline hill and centers on the large central area not yet excavated, embracing the suggestive atmosphere between the old perimeter of ruins and monuments. The composition revolves around the Column of Phocas, the one element to break the central stretch bounded by Santa Maria Nova in the south, the Arch of Titus and the Colosseum in the background.

Left: *Snuffbox with dancer*. Rome (c. 1800?). Tortoise-shell, enamel, gold, miniature mosaic; 4.2 × 3.3 cm (1½ × 1¼ in), Rome, L. Moroni collection. The dancer motif is popular in the neoclassical era following the finds at Herculaneum; the black ground is typical of late sixteenth-century taste, but a certain freedom in the cutting of tesserae and some very lively elements of design and the spatial depth indicate a slightly later date.

Right: *Snuffbox with the Otricoli Jupiter*, by Clemente Ciuli (Rome, documented activity from 1803 to 1828). Rome 1803, signed and dated. Red glass, miniature mosaic; diameter 7.6 cm (3 in). Museo Napoleonico, Rome. The small mosaic adorning the lid shows the famous bust of the Otricoli Jupiter in the Sala Rotonda of the Vatican Museums. On the right, in the lower half of the rim and reading upwards is the inscription: "C. Ciuli Romano F.A. 1803." The snuffbox was given by Pius VII to Prince Joseph Bonaparte, older brother of Napoleon, when the latter was crowned in Paris in 1804. The choice of this and many other objects for dignitaries which the pope would meet on his travels was made by Canova, then inspector general of Fine Arts for the papal state. Canova's artistic acumen is a sign of the high regard for miniature mosaic in the early nineteenth century.

Below: *Two vases*, attributed to Nicola De Vecchis (active 1795–1834). Rome 1795–1800. Marble, hard stones, miniature mosaic; height 51.4 cm (1 ft 8 in), diameter at shoulder 20.7 cm (8¼ in). Los Angeles County Museum of Art, donated by Mr and Mrs Gilbert. Among the earliest miniature mosaics from the Vatican Studio are recorded in 1795 as "two vases in Etruscan style" designed and made by De Vecchis. A pair of vases of simpler structure in statuary marble but with a mosaic frieze like the one described is in a private collection in Rome. This may be a copy by the same artist since both pairs are finely made in perfect neoclassical proportions.

Below: *Table with the Shield of Achilles.* Rome, 1814–1818. Marble, bronze, miniature mosaic; diameter c. 90 cm (3 ft). Versailles Museum, formerly in the Grand Trianon, Versailles. The table top is inspired by Homer's description of Achilles's shield (*Iliad*, book xviii, verses 667–842), giving the complex story in three concentric bands. The mosaic was made by a team from the Vatican Studio (1814–1818) to a cartoon by the Studio's director, Michele Köeck. It was mounted on a supporting foot of four eagles with gilded bronze claws and given by Leo XII to Charles X in 1825.

On pages 284–285: *Table top with head of Jupiter,* by Carlo Montecucchi (active between 1800 and 1900). Florence, 1804, signed and dated. Miniature mosaic; 145 × 73 cm (4 ft 10 in × 2 ft 5¾ in). Pitti Palace, Florence. This piece provides an interesting example of how mosaic art was spreading to other cities. In fact, Carlo Montecucchi worked in Florence in a studio granted to him by the grand duke for a number of years around 1800.

On pages 286–287: *Table with Love's Triumph*. Rome, c. 1820. Mosaic on black stone base; diameter 61 cm (2 ft). Private collection, Rome. The theme of victorious love would appear to be an interpretation of Virgil's "*Omnia vincit Amor*," love conquers all.

Below: *Chimney adorned with mosaics.* Paris, late eighteenth century. Miniature mosaic. Musée du Louvre. Close to the work of the mosaicist Cesare Aguatti, active late seventeenth to early eighteenth century. Similar themes had been used in the Vatican Loggia by Raphael.

FROM TRADITIONAL TO MODERN STYLES

From the high point of Ancient Greece, even during Ancient Egyptian times, mosaic art assumed an important role in architecture. Only in the fifteenth century did it become mostly confined to pavements. The classical wall mosaic, for example, became less and less widespread after the Renaissance to the point that at the beginning of the nineteenth century it seemed forgotten. As if to make up for lost time, mosaic art was revived in a new "renaissance." Naturally enthusiasm was weighed down by the indifferent state of nineteenth-century art, and substantial awakening is only really apparent after 1850. The recovery was more in the technical field rather than the artistic, not so much an art form but *"Une industrie d'art à ressusciter,"* as Eugène Müntz wrote in his essay of 1898.

Nineteenth-century mosaic seems not to aim at individual works but only at accurate reproduction, preserving the memory of fragile frescoes and paintings. This was openly admitted by Antonio Salviati in his account to the jury of the Milan exhibition of 1881, asserting that his workshop could carry out "mosaics on the Roman system which show figures of men and animals, landscapes and so on, by means of small strips of glass admirably joined to make the result look more like a painting. The work is finally smoothed, polished and perfected with a coat of coloured resin to cover the minute gaps and improve the fusion of tints." The few nineteenth-century mosaics confirm that the artists were concerned with imitating painting, trying to hide the true nature of mosaic, as if ashamed of it. These mainly Venetian works aim only at substituting painting with a form that ensured better durability.

The renewed nineteenth-century interest in mosaic is partly due to contemporary fashions in historicist architecture and later in neo-Gothicism, especially in France and England, and then in neo-Romanesque which in Camillo Boito's writings went as far as a national revolution. Meanwhile the Vatican workshop had remained as active in mosaic as it had been since it was set up, except that it received an even greater impetus when Gregory XVI ordered the reproduction of medieval mosaics (fifth to thirteenth century) that decorated the basilica of San Paolo-fuori-le-Mura and were almost completely destroyed in the fire of July 1823. In this climate, Filippo Agricola and Nicola Consoni in 1850–55 produced cartoons for the mosaics of the rebuilt façade of San Paolo. The desire to preserve old fragments continued with the restoration work in Salerno Cathedral in 1873 (and later in 1956) of thirteenth-century mosaics in the bowl-shaped vault of the right apse (Cappella delle Crociate), and with the repair of the mosaic by Iacopo Torriti and Iacopo da Camerino and its installation in the rebuilt apse (1884) of San Giovanni in Laterano in Rome.

About 1850, the South Kensington Museum set up a mosaics workshop on the Roman model, which carried out various mosaics for the Albert Memorial in Kensington Gore and *The Story of St George* in Westminster Palace after cartoons by Edward John Poynter. At the same time in London, Antonio Salviati produced in the pendentives of the cupola of St Paul's Cathedral the mosaics of the Prophets, after cartoons by Alfred Stevens, and the Evangelists after those of Frederick Watts. The mosaics by Clayton and Bell in the Guards Chapel (built in 1838) in Birdcage Walk were destroyed during the Second World War. In 1846, Tsar Nicholas I, inspired by the discovery of eleventh-century Byzantine mosaics in St Sophia in Kiev (among them the famous Virgin as an orant), set up a mosaic school and workshop later transferred to St Petersburg. Here, besides some mosaics for the iconostasis of St Isaac's Cathedral from cartoons by van Neff, many copies of more or less famous pictures were made. The work of this school, first affiliated with imperial manufacture and later with the Academy of Fine Arts, was voluminous throughout the late nineteenth century and till its closure in 1917.

In 1804, in the midst of the neoclassical era, Francesco Belloni set up the Imperial School of Mosaic in Paris, attached after the Restoration to the royal house with the title of Royal Manufacture of Mosaic. In the late nineteenth century, following work at the Opéra which included mosaics from cartoons by the architect of the theater, Charles Garnier, a national school of mosaic opened in Paris. It was directed by Edouard Gerspach, who had been important in its founding, but two years later he left the post to a new director, Poggesi. The main activity of this school was the restoration and imitation of ancient models. One good example is the mosaic by Hébert in the apse of the Panthéon, where the Virgin and Angel who present Joan of Arc and St Genevieve to the enthroned Saviour are based on some of the finest models of mosaic tradition. Likewise modelled on the works of Ravenna are the cartoons of Henri Revoil for the Cathedral of Sainte-Marie-Majeure in Marseilles, begun in 1852 by Léon Vaudoyer, architect also of Notre-Dame-de-la-Garde, with oriental interior mosaic decoration. It was Italian mosaicists who restored the mosaic of Christ and the twenty-four old men in the cupola of Aachen Cathedral in 1882, imitating the destroyed and partly lost originals. The clearest instance of purely technical use of mosaic in the nineteenth-century fashion of merely reproducing paintings, is found in the four large lunettes that decorate the octagon of the Vittorio Emanuele Gallery in Milan. Painted originally in 1867 by Eleuterio Pagliano (*Africa*), Angelo Pietrasanta (*Europe*), Bartolomeo Giuliano (*Asia*) and Raffaele Casnedi (*America*), they were carefully reproduced in mosaic in 1912 when they had seriously deteriorated. The mosaics put together by De Curzon in 1870–75 for the front lobby in the Paris Opéra are charming but mediocre originals. The artist fails to match the showy splendour of Charles Garnier's building, which houses his work. To the same period belong the mosaics by H. Schapper (*Ascent of Calvary* and *Crucifixion*) in the Cathedral of Bremen, and the crowded *Stories* of E. Veit on the façade of the Meissen and Schaden Palace in Vienna. The so-called purism of the Nazarenes is portrayed by Lodovico Seitz in the mosaics of the funeral chapel of Pius IX in the Basilica of San Lorenzo fuori-le-Mura in Rome (1870–75), for which he seemed to draw on the unexceptional models of Overbeck and Cornelius. Round 1900 we have Ludovico Pogliaghi's cartoons for the lunettes (1887) over the three doors of the memorial chapel in the Monumental Cemetery of Milan. They represent allegorical figures (*Genius*, *History* and *Power*) which, despite the artist's undeniable skill, have a feeling of unconvincing rhetoric. In 1903, Pogliaghi created the five allegorical compositions in the funeral chapel of Giuseppe Verdi in the rest home for musicians founded by him in Milan and named after him.

Although, with few exceptions, nineteenth-century mosaics remain sadly mediocre, some useful technical advances were made. These were mostly due to the work of the Vatican mosaic laboratories, particularly in the field of restoration, and to the workshop opened in Murano by Antonio Salviati (1856) which produced numerous mosaics worldwide. The general lull in activity was eventually interrupted by the elegant mosaics (*Tree of Life* and *Annunciation*) of 1896–7 to cartoons by Edward Burne-Jones in the American Church of St Paul in Via Nazionale in Rome. These are not, as some claim, "pre-modern" works, for which the Pre-Raphaelite painter would have felt no sympathy, but brilliant compositions in the style of the period. Here, the result is very successful and proves how suited the work could be, given the right artist.

The change of course in figurative art almost in a cycle over the years, did not occur suddenly. Many forerunners, regrets and nostalgic returns throughout the century unfold the transition from the nineteenth century to the various strands of Art Nouveau. In the art of mosaic there was also a significant turning point precisely in 1900. It was not a move that could be labelled Art Nouveau, nor was it linked with Catalan *Modernismo* in whose territory it became manifest. It was rather a personal and quite individual decision by Antonio Gaudí, much of whose work was in mosaic. As Juan Eduardo Cirlot wrote: "Fourteen years before Victor Horta, in 1878, Antonio Gaudí began architectural modernism in Europe." This is so, provided we do not confuse this sense of "modernism" with that applied to the new Catalan architecture, and confine it to an independent break from the ways and stylistic tricks of an outdated tradition. Mosaics, mostly non-figurative, made up of fragments of coloured stone, marbles and glass, often appear in the jagged coverings, irregular roofing and intricate gables of Gaudí. A profusion of them, and perhaps their best tested application, is in the serpentine balustraded seats of the Parco Güell on Mount Pelada in Barcelona in the years 1900–1914. Some minor structures in the park have coverings, gables, finials and roofs in mosaic whose strong colours, rather than the materials or techniques, recall some Ligurian covering in ceramic tiles.

Though the various new movements (Art Nouveau, Arts and Crafts, *Jugendstil*, *Sezessionstil*, *Stile Liberty* and so on) were widely successful in the western world, the mosaicists who worked at the Sacré-Coeur in Paris from 1912 to 1922 still belonged to an eighteenth-century stylistic climate. Besides the evocative mosaics of *Joan of Arc* and *St Louis* in the Chapelle de l'Armée and those by Maumléjean in the Chapelle des Saints Jésuites, we note the vast and complex mosaic in the choir vault by Henri-Marcel Magne and Luc-Olivier Merson. From cartoons by Merson and Charles Girault, Guilbert Martin executed the mosaics at the Institut Pasteur in Paris, with the allegories of *Charity* in Pasteur's funeral chapel. These mosaics imitate a Byzantine art, aiming at the pseudo-style in which Girault had built the crypt.

In 1901, in a quite different cultural setting, Joseph Maria Olbrich's shining mosaic unfolded on the staircase cupola at the Künstler Kolonie in Darmstadt in a kind of luxurious demonstration of the Viennese Secession. Some typical though late examples of Art Nouveau and its worthy successor, Art Deco, are the 1920 mosaics by Vittorio Emanuele Bressanin on the façade of the Società Salviati building on the Grand Canal in Venice. The elegant ground-level frieze suggests Aristide Sartorio, while the large first floor panel is fussy and unashamedly ingenuous, as it exalts Venice in its prominent role in the Arts. This protraction of Art Nouveau into the 1920s was not unique. Secession and Art Nouveau tastes persisted until around 1925, the year of the great exhibition of Paris under the name of Art Deco.

In a similar period work was going ahead on the mosaics from cartoons by Angioli D'Andrea in the Caffé Camparino in the cathedral square in Milan (1922–5). The mosaic, intended to match the splendid furnishings by Eugenio Quarti, became a wall decoration celebrating the beauty of spring with coloured birds and garlands studded with flowers. D'Andrea's work also differed in technique from nineteenth-century work. The tesserae were no longer square and uniform, but of various shapes and sizes, at times minute, as found in certain details of medieval mosaics. A few years later, mosaic makeup was to adopt irregular hand-cut tesserae of different sizes to match the effect required, as had been the rule in the golden age of mosaic from the sixth to thirteenth centuries. A vague touch of Hungarian folklore marks a cartoon made by Géza Marŏti in 1923–4 for the great mosaic lunette that was intended to evoke the Epochs of Art in the National Theater of Mexico City. The fairy-tale landscapes in the lunettes of the bathroom designed to mark the third Biennial Exhibition of Monza in 1927 hint at the exquisite decorations created by members of the Vienna Workshop under the spirited guidance of Josef Hoffmann. Of these lunettes, as of many other mosaics made on cartoons of Zecchin by the Venetian Mosaic Co-operative under G. Gregorini, only reproductions survive. The mosaics commissioned by Giuseppe Berti in the votive chapel for the Fallen of the Navy in the church of the Madonna del Mare in Pula are, however, extant.

On the model of the Venetian workshop of the Salviatis (now active for fifty years) and of the older Vatican one, the early 1900s saw the opening of two schools for mosaicists, in Spilimbergo and Ravenna. The famous tradition of Venice, Aquileia, Ravenna and the whole former Byzantine province as world supplier of mosaics was thus renewed. Indeed, mosaics all over the world almost always carry the name of mosaicists from Venice or Ravenna, and more particularly from Friuli, even when the cartoons were by foreign artists. For example, mosaicists from Ravenna were employed in Paris and Nice to translate cartoons by Marc Chagall, and in Hamburg for the great *Ecce Homo* by

Oscar Kokoschka in the Church of St Nikolai. In Ravenna, interest in mosaic, even if at first confined to restoration, was revived in the early 1920s, when Count Vittorio Guaccimanni, director of the Academy of Fine Arts, began a course in mosaic there, entrusted to Giovanni Guerrini. On graduating, mosaicist students gathered in a working group called "the Academy of Fine Arts Mosaicists Group" or "Mosaic Workshop." In Friuli, traditional mosaic work, after setbacks, stoppages, complications and resumptions, had more or less survived over the centuries when early in 1922 Lodovico Zanini and the Mayor, Ezio Cantarutti, set up the mosaic school of Spilimbergo, still very active (like its sister schools in the Vatican, Ravenna and Venice) in Italy and, perhaps even more, abroad.

As far as the art of mosaic is concerned, the nineteenth century really ended when the First World War broke out in July 1914, while the new era began over the years 1918 to the start of the Second World War in 1939. The last period that we can mention began in 1945, after the ceasefire, and still continues. The twentieth century can therefore be divided into two unequal but equally coherent parts. Both in Europe, barely recovered from the First World War, and in America, brutally awoken from its long isolation, attempts were made to restore the broken thread of pre-war interests, studies and activities. This was a vain task given that, though little changes over time, nothing repeats itself either and in fact the intense interest in reviving pre-war culture could not produce any significant results.

Currents still alive were Art Nouveau and related styles, the so-called decadent art and the avant-garde movements, Futurism, Cubism and Dadaism. The latter did not make any significant impact except for some delayed reaction after the Second World War, while Futurism and Cubism influenced everything that stemmed from the by now famous and vainly cursed "recall to order" of Waldemar George. The brief season in which the "recall" was both the cause and effect, and from which neither Picasso nor many Scandinavian architects could escape, was significantly but rather inappropriately called "neoclassical." Typical of those years are some mosaics by Giulio Rosso, Pietro D'Achiardi, Giovanni Guerrini and Achille Capizzano, but above all the mosaic floors with labyrinths or in Greek style by Gio Ponti, Tommaso Buzzi and Ottavio Cabiati. The mosaics by Rosso in the Casino of Venice and those (now destroyed) in the Caffé Motta on the cathedral square in Milan, which told the story of bread and *panettone*, are in frank narrative style with a touch of irony. His mosaics reveal the successful outcome of a long experience in decoration, not brilliant but always perfectly elegant.

Distant from Baroque and rather reminiscent of Futurist and Cubist strains are the many mosaics of Gino Severini, including those of 1930 in the Church of Tavannes and in St Pierre in Fribourg and those of 1937 in Padua in Palazzo Liviano and in the Senate Room of the University (*The Tree of Science*). Two features of twentieth-century painting can be found together in the Palazzo dell'Arte in Milan in two mosaics, both made in 1933 for the fifth Triennial Exhibition. One is the *Tre Arti* (the Three Arts) by Severini in the Ceremonial Hall, the other *La Cavalcata delle Amazzoni*, a floor mosaic in the hall at the foot of the staircase, by Leonor Fini from a painted tondo by Achille Funi showing a cavalcade of amazons. Severini's is an archaizing and mysticizing allegory that recalls works by Tullio Garbari and Jacques Maritain's neo-Scholasticism to which Severini and Garbari had come near. Funi's work, on the other hand, clearly and confidently testifies the neoclassicism of the twentieth century. However, both mosaics reveal a desire for renewal. J. Gaudin is not so clearly on this road in his large mosaic *Suffer little Children, and forbid them not, to come unto me*, laid in Paris in Saint-Jean-Baptiste de la Salle in 1935.

Between the two wars, the small mosaic was resumed as a sort of canvas in mosaic, by J. Novàk in Prague (1936), Jeanne Reynal in New York (1941), Guido Marussig in Trieste, and others, such as Domenico Cantatore, Aligi Sassu, Renato Guttuso, Afro and Georges Mathieu. Beyond the clear painterly quality of these small mosaics, we note how they stray from the traditional character and aim of mosaic, which is not bent on portable decoration for domestic interiors but rather on monumental decoration. This was the aim of Angelo Canevari and Achille Capizzano in their floor mosaics in tesserae of black and white marble in the Viale delle Iscrizioni, in Piazzale della Sfera and in the covered swimming pool of the Foro Italico in Rome (1935–37). The same flavour is found in Severini's floor mosaic in Mussolini's gymnasium in the same complex as the covered swimming pool. These are modern interpretations and free inventions somewhat reminiscent of figured pavements in ancient Roman villas and baths.

In this field, the Triennial Exhibition of Milan in the Palazzo dell'Arte had some influence between the wars. It commissioned a series of mosaics by major twentieth-century artists: Funi, Severini, Casorati, Sironi, Campigli and Aldo Salvadori. The works of the last two, shown at the seventh Triennial Exhibition in 1940, were later taken down. Especially noteworthy was Massimo Campigli's mosaic made in marble tesserae by the Venetian G. Padoan on the theme *Peace with Justice*, with two female figures typical of this painter, of Peace protecting a small tree and Justice virtuously splitting a fruit into two halves. The two mosaics by Felice Casorati, *Scene Familiari* (Family Scenes), of unusually rich colour, were finally arranged on the landing of the staircase of the office wing in the Palazzo dell'Arte in Milan. Mario Sironi's mosaic has a more complicated story which is still not concluded. Commissioned for the Triennial of 1936, it was shown there on the central stairs of the Palazzo dell'Arte, but incomplete as only the middle part was ready. When finished, the mosaic was shown in the Italian pavilion at the International Exhibition in Paris in 1937. When returned to Italy, it could not be installed because of work in progress at the Palazzo dell'Arte so it was provisionally placed in the Palazzo dei Giornali in Milan, where it is still waiting for a more suitable home. The mosaic entitled *Lavoro fascista* (Fascist Work), or *Italia Corporativa* (Corporative Italy), was carried out by G. Salviati watched closely by the author who advised on quality, size, cutting and colour of the tesserae, and their direction of placement to achieve certain effects of soft shadows or stronger lights. Equally famous is Sironi's other mosaic, *La Giustizia tra la Legge e la Forza* (Justice between Law and Force), laid in 1936 in the hall of the Court of Assizes in the Palazzo di Giustizia, Milan.

Of the many mosaics planned for the World Exhibition that was to take place in Rome in 1942, most remained at project stage when the War interrupted work. Examples are those for the congress and reception hall, for which cartoons had been prepared by Afro and the group comprising Giovanni Guerrini, Achille Capizzano, Franco Gentilini and Giorgio Quaroni. Among the few realized are floor mosaics on cartoons by Guerrini, Rosso and Severini, placed outside around the fountain in front of the Palazzo degli Uffici, and the second-phase Futurist mosaics made by Fortunato Depero and Enrico Prampolini (1937–38). Depero created a mosaic of 122 square meters in multicoloured stones and different tesserae which is outside the Science Museum and represents the *Professions and the Arts*. The work of Prampolini, on the theme of *The Guilds*, spreads over 190 square meters on the outside of the Museum of arts and crafts. Beyond practical applications for walls or floors, Lucio Fontana successfully ventured into coating sculptures in mosaic, starting with his female plaster busts of the years 1935–1937 and culminating with the *Medusa* of 1940. This covering in plastic features using mosaic work had been tried already by Gaudí in the Güell Park in Barcelona, and later by David Alfaro Siqueiros in the University of Mexico City. In fact, especially in the case of Siqueiros, one might speak of ancestral recollections of pre-Columbian masks with mosaic cover.

The second half of the twentieth century is marked by lively exchanges between Europe and America. This had happened before, but not as often nor with as much effect. This should have been a good thing, but futile experiments and attempts at revival, with both continents trying to take the lead, finally led to an unstable situation with no positive achievements. Initially the more influential achievements went back to a pre-war climate, though developments of increasing interest were emerging. It was the work of restoration and the work by established artists that tied these activities to the first half of the century. Notable restoration of famous monuments was achieved in Venice and Sicily. In Venice, Forlati directed work on restoring the mosaics in St Mark's. In Sicily the restoration of the Roman Villa del Casale in Piazza Armerina was taken up again in 1950 after the initial work begun in 1929 and suspended in 1939. Among the established artists of pre-war years who carried on the mosaic art were Fernand Léger, the ever present Severini, and Siqueiros. These three artists still viewed painting, albeit in accordance with current styles, as communication through images, as a "manifestation" of meaning. Siqueiros, like the other Mexican artists José Clemente Orozco, Diego Rivera and Rufino Tamayo, while often crudely political, succeeded in being highly expressive, with firm and open conviction. In this light we must view the mosaics on cartoons by Siqueiros at the *Rectorado* building of the University of Mexico City. His work proclaims a clear and active revolutionary nationalism. The huge mosaic (1949–57) by Juan O'Gorman on the outside of the bookshop of the university's library, on the other hand, is in a very different vein. Between popular and mythical styles, again, is Eppens's mask for the wall mosaic at the seat of the Society of Venetians of Mexico in Cuernavaca and the gigantic *Raingod* (1952) mosaic on a cartoon by Diego Rivera. The seemingly rough painting of Léger, which is actually very commanding and impressive, above all in the heavy outlines of the figures, was well conveyed in mosaic on the façade of the Musée Léger in Biot, Provence in 1956. The work was commissioned by his widow one year after his death and was taken from an enlarged sketch Léger had prepared for the Olympic stadium in Hanover.

In recent years, the United States has seen a certain zeal for mosaic, with well-known painters like Ben Shahn preparing cartoons for the dreamy mosaic band in the façade of William O'Grady High School in Coney Island, New York. Others, less famous but more prolific, have made cartoons for mosaics, like Max Spivac for the Cerebral Palsy School, Staten Island, New York and the huge composition *Wonders of the World* in the seat of the Charles Pfizer Company in Groton, Connecticut, or Hans Hoffman who produced a large abstract mosaic wall covering in the entrance of the office block at 711 Third Street in New York. Separate mention must be made of the mosaics in the High School of Art and Design of New York, because of the choice simplicity of the figures and certain technical tricks such as using tesserae of various shapes and size (at times considerable), with very effective results.

A vast and ably chosen review of mosaics was organized by Giuseppe Bovini at the Museo Nazionale in Ravenna in 1959. It showed small mosaics, the artistic limitations of which were referred to above, along with many pieces of high quality, particularly those by masters of colour like Georges Mathieu, Bruno Cassinari and Afro. They are able to employ their Venetian connections in so refined and exemplary a use of colour as to abolish the division between figurative, neo-figurative and abstract. Amongst more recent Italian mosaics are the blazing and ingenious floorings where Francesco Somaini has included even bronze tesserae, recapturing the Ravenna tradition of using gold.

In 1928 Adrien Blanchet said that all but a few great modern compositions were unsatisfactory and foretold that this type of decoration, already regarded as lasting forever, must modestly confine itself to ornamentation. Events have more or less happily refuted this, because mosaic's fate, if we must give it one, cannot be separated from that of wall painting or any large decoration. It will inevitably remain an integral part of architectural composition with a deeply meaningful role and a resounding voice accessible to all.

Below: wooden ritual mask covered in turquoise mosaic. Aztec art. Pigorini Museum, Rome. In pre-Columbian America mosaic has a long history. In Peru small objects covered in mosaic of gold, bone, shell and small pieces of ivory were made; excavations at La Venta in Mexico have unearthed floors of the first millennium B.C. of Olmec origin, in which there were pictures of jaguar masks made of pieces of serpentine and coloured ceramics inserted in plaster. In the Zapotec city of Mitla, walls of the ninth century B.C.

have stones arranged in streaks of uniform colour in a geometric pattern. Above all, Mayas and Aztecs specialized in using slim tesserae of semi-precious stones to cover ritual knives, wooden masks and human skulls. Some of these entered European collections even in the Baroque age, but only in modern times, when Gaudí had freed mosaic from its two-dimensional shackles, did these works find a new aesthetic echo. Mexican mosaicists of the twentieth century take great pride in their pre-Columbian heritage.

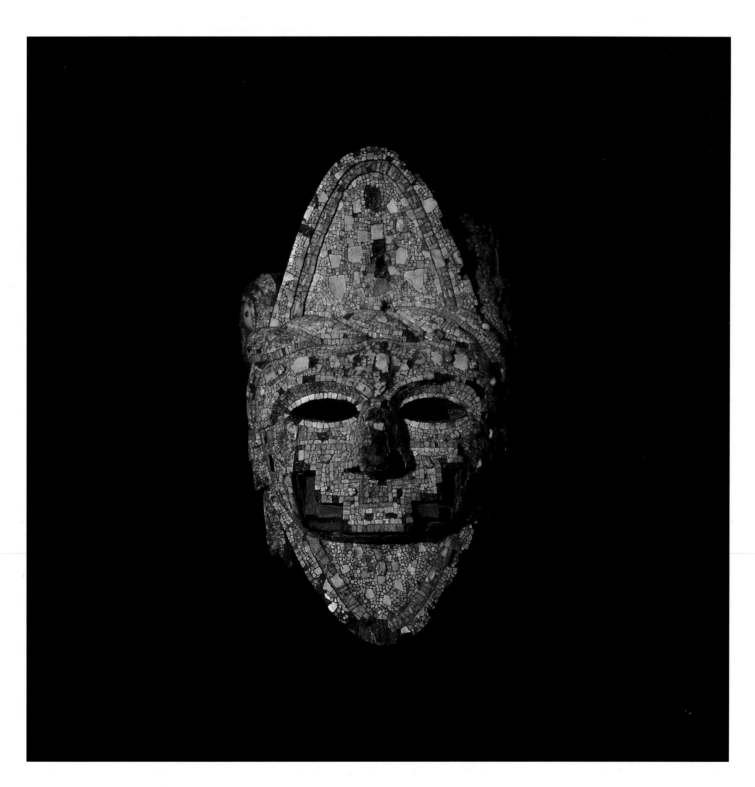

Left: Paris, Opéra. *Orpheus and Eurydice*. Detail of mosaic by Curzon (1870–1875) covering the vault of the front foyer. Made by the Salviati firm of Venice, the subject refers to Gluck's famous opera. On pages 300–301: general view of front foyer, Paris Opéra.

Opposite: Institut Pasteur, Paris, crypt. Allegory of *Charity*. Charles Girault built the crypt in a Byzantine style. Louis Pasteur was buried here in 1895. With Louis-Olivier Merson, Girault also made the cartoons for the mosaics in which the architect's Art Nouveau version of Byzantine is combined in a compromise with the naturalistic style of the painter. The mosaics were executed by Guilbert Martin.

CHARITE

Below and opposite: Sacré-Coeur, Paris, built at Montmartre in 1873 by decree of the National Assembly. It was consecrated in 1919. Amongst its patrons had been Rouhault de Fleury, expert on Christian antiquity. Mosaic played a large part in it. *Joan of Arc* to a cartoon by H. Pinta (opposite), and *Apparition of St Michael* before the island later dedicated to him, on a cartoon by Henry Marcel Magne (below). Early twentieth century. Art Nouveau was thus introduced into church decoration.

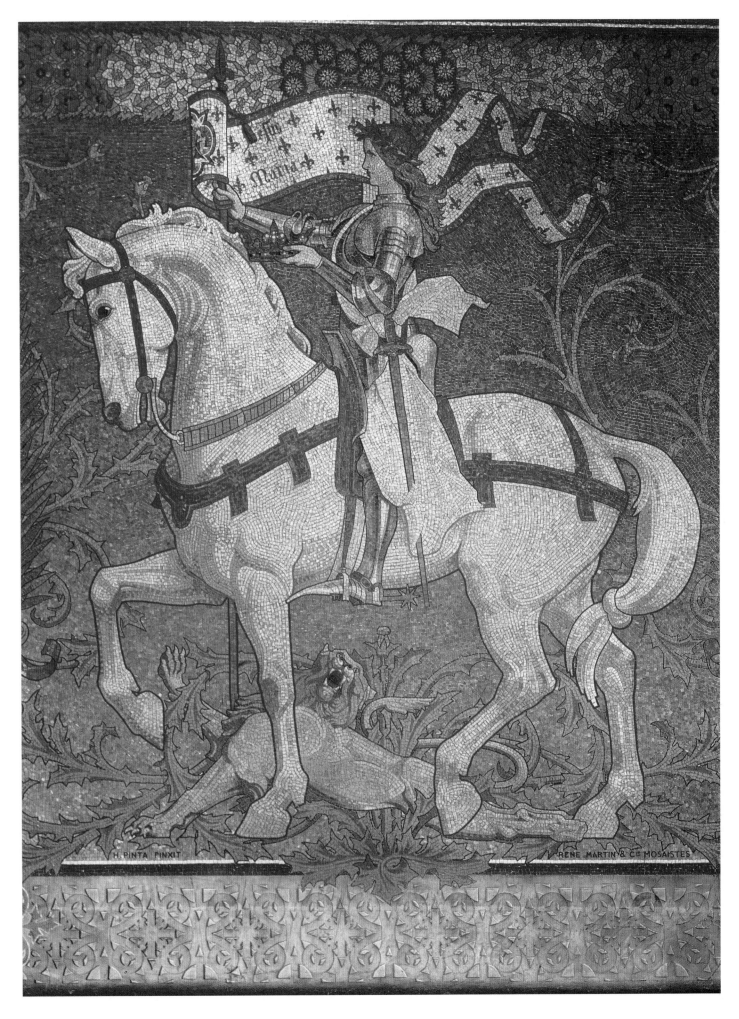

H. PINTA PINXIT

RENE MARTIN & Cⁱᵉ MOSAISTES

303

Opposite: Palace of Westminster, London. Built by Charles Barry and Augustus Pugin in 1835, it was the first British neo-Gothic public building. Pugin in particular was responsible for the rich internal decoration, though work continued into the twentieth century. In this corridor, Victorian statues alternate with frescoes of 1910, while the mosaic with St Stephen Martyr, King Stephen and Edward the Confessor adorn the entrance to St Stephen's Hall, built on the former site of St Stephen's Chapel.

Below: Exhibition Hall, Darmstadt. Cupola of the staircase. Mosaic by J. M. Olbrich.

On pages 306–307: St Paul's, London, *Crucifixion*. In the 1890s a vast scheme of mosaics was undertaken in Wren's magnificent cathedral built between 1675 and 1711. While George Frederick Watts and Alfred Stevens relied on the Italian Renaissance for inspiration for their cartoons, William Richmond aimed at purity and used motifs from medieval Romanesque churches, as in the southwest apse under the great cupola, here shown, recalling twelfth-century mosaics in San Clemente, Rome.

Left and opposite: the American Episcopal Church of St Paul on Via Nazionale in Rome was built in 1879 and named "St Paul within the Walls," underlining the new freedom given to Protestant worship inside the walls of Rome. The architect was George Edward Street, and the interior had mosaics by Edward Burne-Jones, carried out by the Salviati firm of Venice.

In the detail shown opposite, St Catherine (with the wheel) is the wife of Henry Codman Potter, Bishop of New York, St Barbara (with the tower) is Georgiana, wife of the painter, St Cecilia (with the organ) is Mary Dahlgren Astor, wife of the financier William Waldorf Astor, St Dorothy (with the roses) is the daughter of William Morris and finally St Agnes (with the lamb) is Gwendolin Story.

Below: the memorial church of William I (Kaiser-Wilhelm-Gedächtnis-Kirche), in the Zoo quarter of Berlin, was built in 1891–1895 to plans by Franz Schwechten in late Rhenish Romanesque. Very rich for a Protestant church, it had splendid mosaics made by Puhl & Wagner to cartoons by Herman Schaper. Christ the Ruler looks over and protects the Hohenzollern, the ruling family. Contemporary elegance and Byzantine refinement celebrate the historical roots of the monarchy.

Opposite: Cathedral of St Isaac, Leningrad. Mosaic on a cartoon by Van Neff from the mosaic workshop and school started by Nicholas I.

Below and opposite: Güell Park in
Barcelona, built 1905–1914, allowed
Antoni Gaudí to express in exuberant
fashion his vitalistic view of architecture.
Working freely and inspired by garden
architecture, he produced galleries and
stairways linked to Gothic and Spanish
Baroque, with dazzling surfaces covered
in mosaic in ceramic tesserae, as well as
fragments of cups and plates.

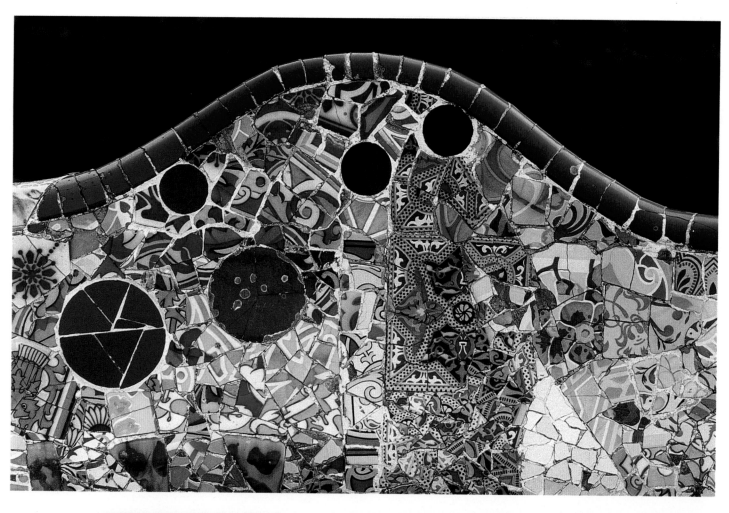

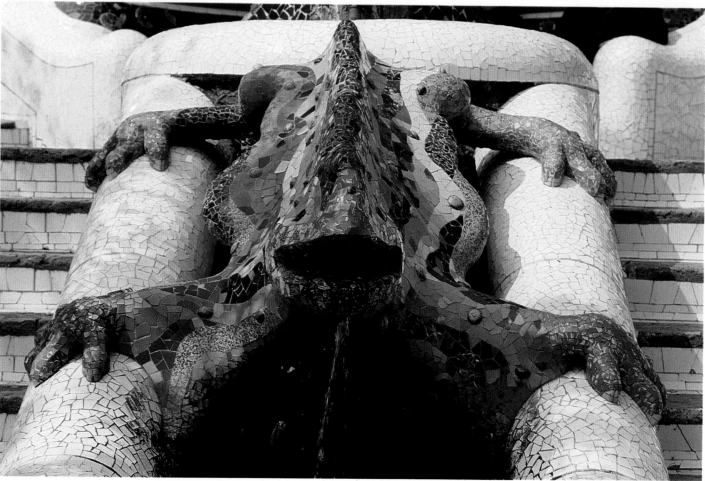

Below: headquarters of the Salviati firm on the Grand Canal, Venice. *Allegory of Venice*, by Vittorio Emanuele Bressanin (1920).

Opposite: Caffé Camparino (now Caffé Zucca), Milan. Detail of floral decoration in mosaic from cartoons by Angiolo D'Andrea (1922–1925).

On pages 316–317: *Waiting* and *Embrace* by Gustav Klimt, Oesterreichisches Museum für Angewandte Kunst, Vienna. In 1905–1909 Klimt executed the great frieze of the dining room in Stoclet House, Brussels. It is clad in white marble and has dark furniture with silver inlays to designs by Josef Hoffmann. The complex work, half inlay and half mosaic, show the Vienna Workshop's mastery and are proof of the artist's ability to exploit different materials and techniques.

315

Opposite: Casino, Lido of Venice. *Scena marina* (Marine scene), by Giulio Rosso.

Below: Palazzo Barbarigo, seat of the Compagnia Venezia Murano, on the Grand Canal. The façade is covered with mosaics from cartoons by Giulio Carlini, in which the ancient art of mosaic is exalted. In the detail shown here, Titian supervises the making by Francesco Zuccato of the mosaic on the central door of St Mark's. This mosaic is actually based on a cartoon by Lorenzo Lotto but we note here the artist's independence as he follows not a cartoon, but only a small drawing.

On pages 320–321: *La Cavalcata delle Amazzoni* (Cavalcade of the Amazons), mosaic by Leonor Fini from cartoons by Achille Funi for the fifth Triennial Exhibition in 1933. Palazzo dell'Arte, Milan.

Right: *Scena familiare* (Family Scene), by Felice Casorati. Palazzo dell'Arte, Milan.

Opposite: *Le Tre Arti* (The Three Arts), by Gino Severini. Mosaic for the fifth Triennial Exhibition. Palazzo dell'Arte, Milan.

On pages 324–325: in 1936, Severini was commissioned to decorate the base of the façade of the new post office in Alessandria, Piedmont (northern Italy). Much later, Umberto Eco would write: "It was a bold gesture, a real idea . . . I have spent days and days thinking about these mosaics, dreaming, embarking on countless adventures between chimney stacks, propellers, turbines, mounted messengers, apes, crocodiles and Aztec monarchs."

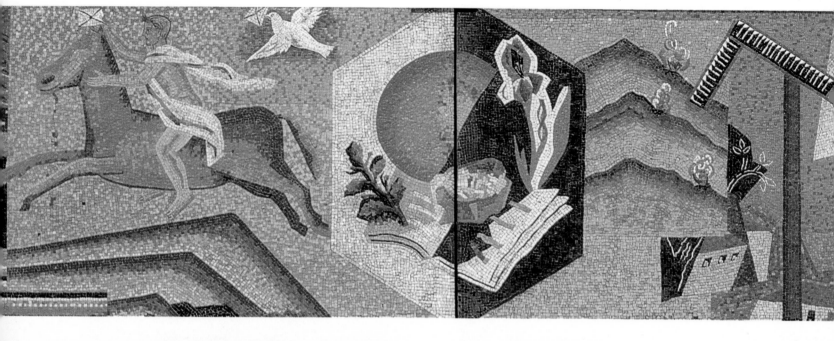

Left and below: Foro Italico, Rome, Piazzale dell'obelisco and Viale delle iscrizioni. Floor mosaics by Angelo Canevari, Achille Capizzano and Giulio Rosso.

On pages 328–329: *La Giustizia fra la Legge e la Forza* (Justice between Law and Force), by Mario Sironi. Palazzo di Giustizia, Milan.

Below: in 1941, Enrico Prampolini, head of the second Futurist school, created a large mosaic outside the Museum of arts and crafts at the EUR (Esposizione Universale di Roma), Rome. An elegant abstract design absorbs heraldic and propaganda motifs, with a subtle gradation of colour that does not overwhelm the architecture.

Opposite: *Suffer little children, and forbid them not, to come unto me.* Saint-Jean-Baptiste de la Salle, Paris. The church was built by the architect Jacquemin in 1908–10. The mosaic decoration is by Jean Gaudin, who created this scene in the choir in 1935.

LAISSEZ VENIR A MOI LES PETITS ENFANTS

Below: Faculty of Medicine, University,
Mexico City. Mosaic by Eppens.

Opposite: University Library, Mexico
City. Mosaics by Juan O'Gorman,
1951–1953. Spanish heraldry, magic
books and Mayan hieroglyphs, reference
to the dead Aztec world and the popular
cultures of modern Mexico sum up the
wisdom gathered here.

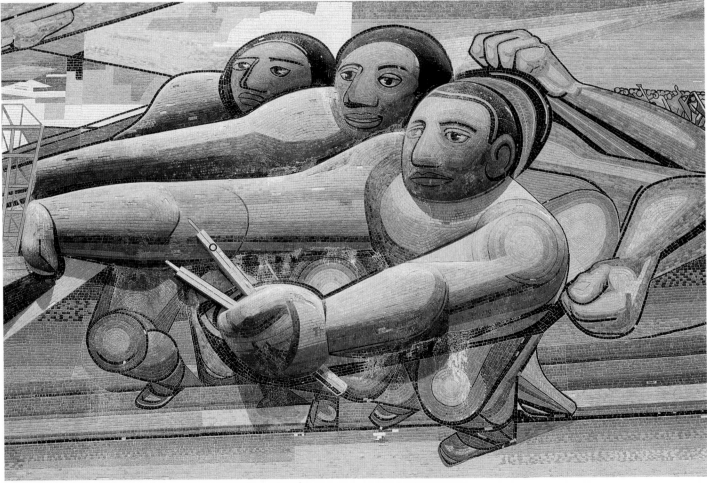

Opposite: *Rectorado* building, University, Mexico City. *El pueblo a la Universidad, la Universidad al pueblo* (The people to the University, the University to the people.) Mosaic bas-relief by David Alfaro Siqueiros (1952–1956).

Right: Faculty of Medicine, University, Mexico City. Mosaic by Eppens. The stylized Mexican motifs of the corn, the plumed serpent and the Aztec mask are heraldic figures on a monumental scale.

Right: Horton Plaza, San Diego, California. Column clad in mosaic.

Below: Musée Léger, Biot, France. On
the façade a mosaic after a model by
Léger for the Olympic stadium of
Hanover (1956).

Left: Faculty of Law, University of Nice. *Ulysses and Nausicaa*. Mosaic by Lino Melano from a cartoon by Marc Chagall (1967).

Below: *Uomini del sud* (Men of the
South), by Domenico Cantatore (in the
artist's collection). He wished to
introduce into the irregularity of tesserae
the rough texture typical of modern oil
painting.

Opposite: *Crucifixion*, from a cartoon by
Oskar Kokoschka. Sankt Nikolai,
Hamburg. The rich colour of
Kokoschka's style seems to translate
successfully into mosaic.

Below: *Female bust*, by Lucio Fontana. Plaster covered in mosaic. Fondazione Fontana, Milan.

Opposite: *La preghiera della sera* (Evening Prayer). Marble and glass mosaic by Luigi Spacal; 104 × 78 cm (3 ft 5½ in × 2 ft 7 in), 1988, executed by Luca Pessoli.

343

Below: abstract mosaic decoration by Hans Hoffman. Entrance to a block in Third Street, New York.

Opposite and on pages 346–347: details from the mosaic panel from cartoons by Ben Shahn on the façade of William O'Grady High School, Coney Island, New York.

Below: floor mosaic in the foyer of the
Teatro Filodrammatici, Milan.

Below: floor mosaic of the Galleria Strasburgo, Milan. Francesco Somaini, 1959.

On pages 350–351: Albissola marina (Savona). Details of the floor mosaic *Passeggiata degli Artisti* (The Artists' walk). Unique work of its kind, highly coloured and suggestive, produced by twenty artists of the second futurist generation, each with a new and original creation. The twenty sections are in coloured glass tesserae making up an unusual mosaic work almost 800 m (c. 2,600 ft) long over an area of some 1,000 sq m (c. 10,800 sq ft).

On page 352: *Oggi dodicesimo giorno del quarto mese dell'anno uno, nove, otto, otto . . .* (Today twelfth day of the fourth month of the year one, nine, eight, eight . . .) by Alighiero Boetti. Mosaic in glass tesserae, 140 × 62 cm (4 ft 8 in × 1 ft 9 in). In this panel, completed in 1988 in conjunction with the masters of the Mosaic Co-operative of Ravenna, the conceptual painter finds a happy fusion of spray painting, which is part of his typical painting output, and the devices of older mosaic tradition: a white ground and free play in arranging the tesserae.

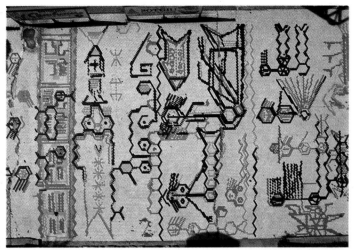

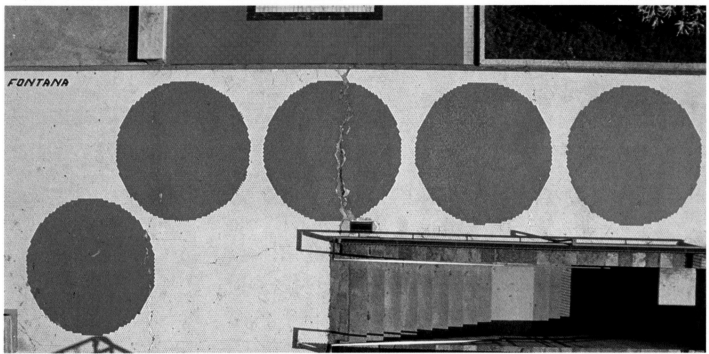

351

352

Bibliography

ANCIENT MOSAICS

ARTAUD, F. *Histoire abrégée de la peinture en mosaïque*, Lyons 1835.
BLAKE, M. E. *Memoirs of the American Academy at Rome*, VIII, 1930, pp. 7 and ff.; XIII, 1936, pp. 67 and ff.; XVII, 1940, pp. 81 and ff.
MOREY, C. R. *The Mosaics of Antioch*, New York 1938.
PERNICE, E. *Die hellenistische Kunst in Pompeji*, VI, *Pavimente und Mosaiken*, Berlin 1938.
LEVI, D. *Antioch Mosaic Pavements*, Princeton 1947.
GULLINI, G. *I mosaici di Palestrina*, Rome 1955.
PACE, B. *I mosaici di Piazza Armerina*, Rome 1955.
GENTILI, G. V. *La villa erculea di Piazza Armerina, I mosaici figurati*, Milan 1959.
PARLASCA, E. *Die römischen Mosaiken in Deutschland*, Berlin 1959.
AVI-YONAH, M. *Israele, mosaici pavimentali antichi*, Paris 1960.
BECATTI, G. *Gli scavi di Ostia*, IV, *I mosaici*, Rome 1961.
LEVI, D. *Mosaico*, nella "Enciclopedia dell'arte antica, classica e orientale" V, Rome 1963, pp. 209–240.
BRUNEAU, P. *Explorations Archéologiques de Délos*, XXIX, *Les Mosaïques*, Paris 1972.
Corpus de los mosaicos romanos de España, I, "Mosaicos romanos de Merida", di A. B. Freijerio, Madrid 1978.
FERNANDEZ CASTOR, M. *Villas Romanas en España*, Madrid 1982.
DASZEWSKI, W. A. *Corpus of Mosaics from Egypt*, I, *Hellenistic and Early Roman Period*, Mainz 1985.
Since 1963 there have been occasional conventions dedicated to the study of ancient mosaics. The records of these have become an invaluable source of information for historical and critical discussion. The following volumes are already published:
IIe Colloque International pour l'étude de la mosaïque antique, organisé par H. Stern et M. Le Geay, Vienna 1971, Paris 1975, "Colloques Internationaux du Centre National de la Recherche Scientifique, Sciences Humaines".
III Colloquio Internazionale sul mosaico antico, Ravenna 1980, ed. by R. Farioli Campanati, Ravenna 1984, "Università degli Studi di Bologna, Istituto di Antichità Ravennati e Bizantine, Association Internationale pour l'Etude de la Mosaïque Antique (AIEMA)".
Begun 1909 l'*Inventaire des mosaïques de la Gaule et de l'Afrique* (I, Gaule; III Algérie); in 1957 became *Recueil des mosaïques de la Gaule* (I, *Belgique*).

CHRISTIAN MOSAICS

MONNERET DE VILLARD, U. *I dati storici relativi a mosaici pavimentali cristiani di Lombardia*, "Archivio storico lombardo", XLIII, 1916, pp. 341–392.
FASIOLO, O. *I mosaici d'Aquileia*, Rome 1915.
GNIRS, A. *Die christliche Kultanlage aus konstantinischer Zeit am Platz des Domes von Aquileia*, Vienna 1915.
WILPERT, J. *Die römischen Mosaiken und Malereien der kirchlichen Bauten vom IV bis zum XIII Jahrhundert*, Freiburg 1917.

VAN BERCHEM, M.-CLOUZOT, E. *Mosaïques chrétiennes du IV aux X siècle*, Geneva 1924.
VENTURI, A. *Mosaici cristiani di Roma*, Florence 1925.
RICCI, C. *Tavole storiche dei mosaici di Ravenna*, Rome 1930–35.
HINKS, J. P. *Catalogue of the Greek, Etruscan and Roman Paintings and Mosaics in the British Museum*, London 1933.
ANTHONY, E. W., *A History of Mosaics*, Boston 1935.
BETTINI, S. *La pittura bizantina*, I, "Mosaici", Florence 1939.
BLAKE, M. E. *Mosaics of the Late Empire in Rome and Vicinity*, MAA Rome, XVII, 1940.
LEVI, D. *Antioch Mosaic Pavements*, Princeton 1947.
DEICHMANN, F. W. *Frühchristliche Kirchen Roms*, Basel 1948.
DEMUS, O. *Byzantine Mosaic Decoration*, London 1948.
LASAREFF, V. *Istorija vizantijskoj zivopisi* (History of Byzantine painting), Moscow 1948.
FROLOW, A. *La mosaïque murale byzantine*, Bizantinoslavica, XII, 1951, p. 180 ff.
GRABAR, A. *La peinture byzantine*, Geneva 1953.
KOLLWITZ, J. *Mosaiken*, Freiburg i.B., 1953.
WEIDLE, W. *Mosaici paleocristiani e bizantini*, Milan-Florence, 1954.
PACE, B. *I mosaici di Piazza Armerina*, Rome 1955.
CECCHELLI, C. *I mosaici della basilica di S. Maria Maggiore*, Turin 1956.
GENTILI, G. V. *La villa imperiale di Piazza Armerina*, Rome 1956.
KAHLER, H. *Die spätantiken Bauten unter dem Dom von Aquileia und ihre Stellung innerhalb der Geschichte des frühchristlichen Kirchenbaues*, Saarbrücken 1957.
LASSUS, J. *Réflexions sur la mosaïque*, Algiers, 1957.
ZOVATTO, L. *Monumenti paleocristiani di Aquileia e Grado*, Udine 1957.
BOVINI, G. *Mosaici di S. Apollinare Nuovo di Ravenna*, Florence 1958.
DEICHMANN,. F. W. *Frühchristliche Bauten und Mosaiken von Ravenna*, Baden-Baden 1958.
STERN, H. *St. Costanza*, "Dumbarton Oaks Papers", XII, 1958, pp. 157–218.
GENTILI, G. V. *La villa Erculia di Piazza Armerina*, Rome 1959.
L'ORANGE, H. P., - NORDHAGEN, P. J. *Mosaik von der Antike bis zum Mittelalter*, Munich 1960.
BECATTI, G. *Scavi di Ostia*, "I mosaici", Rome 1961.
BOVINI, G. *Principale bibliografia su Ravenna romana, paleocristiana e paleobizantina. Corsi di cultura sull'arte ravennate e bizantina*, Ravenna 1961, pp. 1–35.
CAGIANO DE AZEVEDO, M. *I proprietari della villa di Piazza Armerina*, "Studi in onore di M. Salmi", Rome 1961.
MATTHIAE, G. *Le chiese di Roma dal IV al X secolo*, 2 vol., Rome 1962.
BOVINI, G. *Mosaico*. In "Enciclopedia Universale dell'Arte", Rome-Florence 1976, pp. 698 ff.
OAKESHOTT, W. *The Mosaics of Rome*, London 1967.
BRENK, B. *Die frühchristlichen Mosaiken in S. Maria Maggiore zu Rom*, Wiesbaden 1975.
KITZINGER, B. *Byzantine Art in the Making, Main Lines of Stylistic development in Mediterranean Art, 3rd–7th Century*, Harvard University Press, Cambridge, Ma. 1980

BERTELLI, C. *I mosaici*, in *La basilica di S. Lorenzo in Milano* (various authors), Milan 1985, pp. 145–170.

NORDHAGEN, P. J. *I mosaici in Sant'Aquilino*, in "Il millennio ambrosiano", ed. by C. Bertelli, I, Milan 1987, pp. 162–177.

BYZANTINE MOSAICS

SCHULTZ, R. W. - BARNSLEY, S. H. *The Monastery of Saint Luke in Phokis*, London 1901.

LE TOURNEAU, M. - SALADIN H. *Les monuments chrétiens de Salonique*, Paris 1918.

SCHMIT, TH. *Die Koimesis-Kirche von Nikaia*, Berlin-Leipzig 1927.

DIETZ, E. - DEMUS, O. *Byzantine Mosaics in Greece, Hoios David and Daphni*, Cambridge, Mass. 1931.

WHITTEMORE, TH. *The mosaics of St. Sophia at Istanbul*, I–IV, Oxford 1933–1952.

WATZINGER, C. *Denkmaler Palastinas*, II, Leipzig 1935, pp. 107–116.

SOTIRION, G. A. AND M. G. *The basilika ton hagion Demetrion Thessalonikes*, Athens 1952.

STERN, H. *Les representations des Conciles dans l'église de la Nativité à Bethléem*, "Byzantion", XI, 1936, p. 101, XIII, 1938, p. 82, IX, 1957, p. 141.

TALBOT RICE, D. *Les mosaïques du grand palais des empereurs byzantins à Costantinople*, "RArts", V, 1955, pp. 159–166.

BAGATTI, b. *Il significato dei mosaici della scuola di Madaba*, RACr, XXXIII, 1957, pp. 139–160.

LEROY, J. *Mosaïques funéraires d'Edessa*, Syria, XXXIV, 1957, pp. 306–342.

KITZINGER, E. *Byzantine Art in the period between Justinian and Iconoclasm*, Berichte zum XI. "Internationalen Byzantinisten-Kongress", IV, I, Munich 1958.

MACANLAY, W. J. - STEVENSON, R. B. - BRETT, G. - TALBOT RICE, D. - *The Great Palace of the Byzantine Emperors*, 2 vol., Edinburgh 1947, 1958.

MANGO, C. A. *The mosaics of St. Sophia at Istanbul*, Washington 1962.

UNDERWOOD, P. A., *The Kariye Djami*, 3 vol., New York 1966.

KITZINGER, E. *Mosaic Pavements in the Greek East and the Question of a "Renaissance" under Justinian*, in "Actes du VIe Congrès international d'études byzantines", II, Paris 1951, pp.209 ff., now in Kitzinger E., *The art of Byzantium*, Bloomington-London 1976.

LAZAREF, V. *Mozaiki Sofii Kievskoi* (*The St. Sophia mosaics at Kiev*), Moscow.

FORSYTH G. H. - WEITZMANN, K. *The Monastery of Saint Catherine at Mount Sinai: The Church and the Fortress of Justinian*, n.d.

BYZANTINE PORTATIVE MOSAICS

MÜNTZ, E. *Les mosaïques portatives*, in "Bulletin Monumental", LII, Caen 1886, pp. 233 and ff.

RICE, D. T. *New Light on Byzantine Portative Mosaics*, in "Apollo", XVIII, 1933, pp. 265 and ff.

BETTINI, S. *Appunti per lo studio dei mosaici portatili bizantini*, in "Felix Ravenna", XLVI, 1938–41, pp. 7 and ff.

DEMUS, O. *Byzantinische Mosaikminiaturen*, in "Phaidros", III, 1947, pp. 190 and ff.

FELICETTI-LIEBENFELS, W. *Geschichte der byzantinischen Ikonenmalerei von ihren Anfängen bis zum Ausklange unter Berücksichtigung der Maniera gresa und der Italobyzantinischen*, Olten-Lausanne 1956.

DEMUS, O. *Two Palaeologan Mosaic Icons in the Dumbarton Oaks Collection*, in "Dumbarton Oaks Papers", XIV, 1960, pp. 89 and ff.

Byzantine Art, a European Art. Catalogue of the Council of Europe exhibition, Athens 1964.

BERTELLI, C. *The Image of Pity, in Santa Croce in Gerusalemme*, in "Essays in the History of Art Presented to R. Wittkower", London 1967.

BANK, A. *Byzantine Art in the Collection of Soviet Museums*, 2nd ed. Leningrad 1977.

WEITZMANN ET AL. *Le icone*, Milan 1981.

MEDIEVAL MOSAICS

GERSPACH, E. *La mosaïque*, Paris n.d. (1899).

WILPERT, J. *Die römischen Mosaiken und Malereien der kirchlichen Bauten von IV bis XIII Jahrhundert*, Freiburg in Breisgau 1917.

VAN BERCHEM, M. *The mosaics of the Dome of the Rock at Jerusalem and of the Great Mosque at Damascus*, in Creswell, *Early Muslim architecture*, I, Oxford 1932, pp. 149–252.

DEMUS, O. *The mosaics of Norman Sicily*, London 1949.

SALVINI, R. *Mosaici medievali in Sicilia*, Florence 1949.

I mosaici del Battistero di Firenze, 5 vol., Florence 1954.

KITZINGER, E. *I mosaici di Monreale*, Palermo 1960.

DEGANI, M. *I mosaici romanici di Reggio Emilia*, Reggio E. 1961.

HUECK, I. *Das Programm der Kuppelmosaiken in Florentiner Baptisterium*, Mondorf/Rhein 1962.

BOTTARI, S. *Mosaici bizantini della Sicilia*, Milan 1963.

WAETZOLD, S. *Die kopien des 17. Jahrhunderts nach Mosaiken und Wandmalereien in Rom*, Vienna 1964.

VAN BERCHEM, M. - CLOUZOT, E. *Mosaïques chrétiennes du IVe au Xe siècle*, Geneva 1924 (new ed. Rome 1965).

KARPP, H. *Die frühchristlichen und mittelalterlichen Mosaiken in S. Maria Maggiore zu Rom*, Baden-Baden 1966.

MATTHIAE, G. *Pittura romana del Medioevo*, Rome 1966.

DAKESHOTT, W. *The mosaics of Rome from the 3rd to the 14th centuries*, London 1967.

MATTHIAE, G. *Mosaici medievali delle chiese di Roma*, Rome 1967.

BERTAUX, E. *L'art dans l'Italie méridionale*, I, Paris 1904 (new ed. Rome 1968).

KIER, H. *Der mittelalterliche Schmuckfussboden*, Düsseldorf 1970.

GLASBERG, V. *Répertoire de la mosaïque médiévale pariétale et portative*, Amsterdam 1974.

STERN, H. *Les mosaïques de la Grande Mosquée de Cordove*, in "Madrider Forschungen", 11, Berlin 1976.

HAUG, W. *Das Mosaik von Otranto, Darstellung, Dentung und Bilddokumentation*, Wiesbaden 1977.

BARRAL I ALTET, X. *Els mosaics de paviment medievals a Catalunya*, in "Artestudi. Art romanic", 10, Barcelona 1979.

GLASS, D. *Studies on Cosmatesque pavements*, in "BAR international series", 82, Oxford 1980.

WILLEMSEN, C. D. *L'enigma di Otranto. Il mosaico pavimentale del presbiterio di Pantaleone nella Cattedrale*, Bari 1980.

BARRAL I ALTET, X. *Les mosaïques de pavement médiévales de Venise, Torcello et Murano*, Bibliothèque des Cahiers archéologiques, Paris 1982.

DEMUS, O. *The mosaics of San Marco in Venice*, 4 vol., Chicago-London 1984.

CASTELNUOVO, E. (ed.) *La pittura in Italia, Il Duecento e il Trecento*, Milan 1985.

RIZZARDI, C. *Mosaici altoadriatici. Il rapporto artistico Venezia - Bisanzio - Ravenna in età medievale*, Biblioteca di Felix Ravenna, Ravenna 1985.

Claussen, P. C. *Magistri Doctissimi romani, Die römischen Marmorkünstler des Mittelalters. Corpus Cosmatorum I*, in

"Forschungen zur Kunstgeschichte und christliche Archeologie",
14 Stuttgart 1987.
BARRAL I ALTET, X *Les mosaïques de pavement médiévales en France et
en Italie*, Rome.

RENAISSANCE MOSAICS

ALBERTINI, F. *Opusculum de mirabilibus novae et veteris urbis Romae*,
Rome 1510.
VASARI, G. *Le vite de' più eccellenti pittori, scultori e architetti*,
Florence 1568, *Proemio, I, Dell'architettura*, chapters V and VI; 2,
Della pittura, chapter XV.
CELIO, G. *Memoria delli nomi dell'artefici delle pitture che sono in
alcune chiese, facciate e palazzi di Roma*, Rome 1638, p. 81.
MILANESI, G. *Dell'arte del vetro per musaici, tre trattati dei secoli XIV
e XV*, Bologna, 1864.
FUMI, L. *Il duomo di Orvieto e i suoi restauri*, Rome 1891.
SACCARDO, P. *Les mosaïques de Saint-Marc de Venise*, Venice 1896.
BUSIRI VICI, A. *Il celebre studio del mosaico*, Rome 1901.
FIOCCO, G. *Il rinnovamento toscano dell'arte mosaico a Venezia*, in
"Dedalo", VI, 1925, pp. 109 and ff.
CHASTEL, A. *La mosaïque à Venise et à Florence au XVe siècle* in
"Arte Veneta" VIII, 1954, pp. 119–130 (republished in A.
Chastel, *Favole, forme, figure*, Turin 1988, pp. 69–81).
MURARO, M. *L'esperienza di Paolo Uccello*, in "Atti del XVIII
Congresso Internazionale di Storia dell'Arte", Venice 1956, p.
197.
PET' AS, F. *Das Jungste Gericht, Mittelalterliches Mosaik vom Prager
Veitsdom*, Prague 1958.
HARTT, F. *The Earliest Works of Andrea del Castagno*, in "Art
Bulletin" XLI, 1959, pp. 151–181 and 225–236.
Muraro, M. *The Statutes of the Venetian Arti and the Mosaics of the
Mascoli Chapel*, in "Art Bulletin", LXII, 1961, pp. 263–274.
CARLI, E. *Il duomo di Orvieto*, Rome 1965, pp. 79–97.
FROMMEL, C. L. *Baldassare Peruzzi als Maler und Zeichner*, in
"Beiheft zum Römischen Jahrbuch für Kunstgeschichte" XI,
Vienna Munich 1967–68.
D'ONOFRIO, C. - PIETRANGELI, C. *Le abbazie del Lazio*, Rome 1969,
pp. 189–90.
MERKEL, E. *Un problema di metodo: la "Dormitio Virginis" dei
Mascoli*, in "Arte Veneta", XXVII, 1973, pp. 65–80.
DI FEDERICO, F. R. *The Mosaics of Saint Peter's Decorating the new
Basilica*, University Park, The Pennsylvania State University
Press, 1983.
BENTIVOGLIO, E. *La Cappella Chigi*, in *Raffaello architetto*, ed. by
C. L. Frommel, S. Ray, M. Tafuri, Milan 1984, pp. 125 and ff.
DEMUS, O. *The mosaics of Saint Mark's*, Washington D.C. 1986, pp.
1–15.
ORTOLANI, S. *Santa Croce in Gerusalemme*, Le Chiese di Roma
illustrate, 106, Rome, n.d. p. 66

EIGHTEENTH-CENTURY MOSAICS

GUATTANI, G. A. *Memorie Enciclopediche delle Antichità e Belle Arti
di Roma*, Rome 1806–1819.
FUMI, L. *Il duomo di Orvieto e i suoi restauri*, Rome 1891.
SACCARDO, P. *Les mosaïques de Saint Marc*, Venice 1895.
GERSPACH, E. *La Mosaïque*, Paris n.d. (1899).
BUSIRI VICI, A. *Il celebre studio del mosaico*, Rome 1901.
HAUTECOEUR, L. *I mosaicisti sampietrini del '700*, in "L'Arte", XIII,
1910, p. 450 ff.
BLANCHET, A. *La mosaïque*, Paris 1928.

EFIMOVA, E. *West European Mosaic of the 13th–19th Centuries in the
Collection of the Hermitage*, Leningrad 1968.
WATERMAN, E. A. *History of mosaics*, New York 1968.
DI FEDERICO, F. R. *Francesco Trevisani. Eighteenth Century Painter
in Rome*, Washington D.C. 1977.
GONZALES-PALACIOS, A. *The Art of Mosaics. Selections from the
Gilbert Collection*, Los Angeles County Museum of Art, Los
Angeles 1977. (This and the author's other works were the first
pieces of research dealing specifically with privately
commissioned mosaics and miniature mosaics, and have proved
vital starting points for research.)
DI FEDERICO, F. R. *The Mosaic Decorations for the Chapel of the Choir
in Saint Peter's*, in "Storia dell'Arte", 1978, n. 32, pp. 71–81.
PIETRANGELI, C. *Mosaici in piccolo*, in "Bollettino dei Musei
Comunali di Roma", 1978–80, n. 1–4, p. 83 ff.
PETOCHI, D. - ALFIERI, M. - BRANCHETTI, M. G. *I Mosaici Minuti
Romani dei secoli XVIII e XIX*, Sesto Fiorentino 1981. (Also
contains a biographical index of the mosaicists working in Rome
between 1727 and 1900.)
GONZALES-PALACIOS, A. *Mosaici e pietre dure*, I, Milan 1982.
PIETRANGELI, C. *Pio VII a Firenze e a Parigi nel 1804–5: doni del
Papa*, in "L'Urbe" n. 5, 1982, pp. 169–177.
PIETRANGELI, C. *Gioacchino Falcioni scultore e mosaicista romano*, in
"Strenna dei romanisti", 1983, pp. 377–384.
ALFIERI, M. - BRANCHETTI, M. G. - CORNINI, G. (ed.) *I Mosaici
minuti romani del '700 e dell' '800*, Catalogue of Exhibition in
Rome, Braccio di Carlo Magno, Vatican; Città di Castello
1986.

NINETEENTH- AND TWENTIETH-CENTURY MOSAICS

DIDRON, E. *Du rôle décoratif de la peinture en mosaïque*, in "Gazette
des Beaux-Arts", Paris 1875, pp. 442–459.
SALVIATI, A. *La Manifattura Salviati per mosaici e vetri all'Esposizione
industriale italiana 1881 a Milano*, Milan 1881.
FANTONI, FILIPPINI, A. *L'Arte del mosaico a Venezia*, in
"Emporium", Bergamo 1896.
MÜNTZ, E. *Une industrie d'art à ressusciter*, Paris 1898.
FURNIVAL, W. J. *Leadless Decorative Tiles, Faience and Mosaics*,
Staffordshire 1904.
JEAN, R. *Les arts de la terre*, Paris 1911.
AGAZZI, A. *Il mosaico in Italia. Raccolta di note storiche e tecniche*,
Milan 1926.
MARANGONI, G. *Decorazione murale, pietre lavorate, mosaico,
pavimento artistico*, Milan 1928. (vol. IV of "Enciclopedia delle
moderne arti decorative italiane").
WATHMAN, E. *A History of Mosaics*, Boston 1935, New York 1968.
PAGANO, G. *Arte decorativa italiana*, Milan 1938.
KING, A. H. *Mosaic and allied Techniques*, Los Angeles 1940.
SEVERINI, G. *Mosaico et arte murale nell'antichità e nei tempi moderni*,
in "Felix Ravenna", Ravenna 1950, n. LX, pp. 21–37 (reprinted
in: G. Mascherpa, *Severini e il mosaico*, 1985).
YOUNG, J. *Course in Making Mosaics*, New York 1957.
ARGIRO, L. *Mosaic Art Today*, Scranton/Pennsylvania 1961.
FISCHER, P. *Das Mosaik, Entwichlung. Technik. Eigenart*, Vienna-
Munich 1969.
FIORENTINI RONCUZZI, I. *Arte e tecnologia del mosaico*, Ravenna
1971.
MASCHERPA, G. *Severini e il mosaico*, Ravenna 1985.
BOVINI, G. - ARGAN, G. C. - PORTOGHESI, P. - FISCHER, P., *Mosaici
d'artisti contemporanei*, Ravenna 1986.
I mosaici di Afro, Catalogue of exhibition in Milan held in the
Galleria Annunciata, Milan 1987.
MINARDI, B. *Casa di mosaico*, in "Domus", Milan 1988, p. 16.

Index

Picture credits

A.F.E., Rome: 21, 66–67, 68–69, 78–79, 80–81, 83, 84, 85, 125, 148, 184–185, 186–187, 250, 277, 279 (L. Canali); 22, 23, 33, 297 (G. Tomsich); 256, 312, 313 (E. Martino); 276 (A. De Luca). Claudio Angeleri, Alessandria: 324–325. Archivio Mondadori, Milan: 28, 36, 203, 336, 337. Art Resource, New York: 332, 333, 335. Museo del Bardo, Tunis: 38, 39. Xavier Barral, Paris: 178, 179, 182. Daniele Casadio, Ravenna: 343, 352. Elio Ciol, Casarsa: 29, 61, 183, 190, 198, 199, 202, 311. Pasquale De Antonis, Rome: 53. Photoservice Fabbri, Milan: 130, 131, 132–133, 134–135, 136–137, 138, 139, 140, 141, 142–143, 144, 145, 146–147, 149, 150–151, 162, 177, 188, 206–207, 209, 270, 271, 283, 284–285, 288, 305, 328–329, 334, 338–339, 340. F.M.R., Milan: 26–27, 90–91, 92–93, 152, 153, 154, 155, 255, 286–287 (M. Listri); 200–201, 274–275, 308, 309 (A. De Luca). Paolo Folchitto, Rome: 281b, 330. Vincent Foscato, New York: 344, 345, 346–347. Foto Giacomelli, Venice: 204–205, 238, 239, 242–243, 248–249, 318. Marianne Haller, Vienna: 273. I.C.P., Milan: 17, 20, 40, 41, 82, 114, 121, 128, 191, 192, 246, 247. Studio Ikona (Papanicolaou-Kaidemenos), Salonika: 113, 115, 116–117, 118, 119, 122, 123, 124, 126, 127, 159. Hubert Josse, Paris: 299, 302, 303, 331. Kaiser Wilhelm Gedächtnis Kirche, Berlin: 310. The Los Angeles County Museum of Art: 282. Franco Marzi, Rome: 266, 267, 268. Jacques Moatti, Paris: 298, 300–301. Foto Nadia Murgioni, Rome: 278, 280, 281a, 326, 327. Karel Neubert, Prague: 236–237. Toni Nicolini, Milan: 30–31, 32, 44, 252–253, 320–321, 322, 323, 342, 348, 349. Kazuyoshi Nomachi, Tokyo: 120–121; Olympia, Milan: 315. Piero Orlandi, Lainate: 254. Oroñoz, Madrid: 196. Karl-Heinz Petersen, Hamburg: 341. Photobusiness, Leopoldsdorf: 316, 317. Studio Piccardo & Rosso, Savona: 350–351. Agenzia Laura Ronchi, Milan: 224, 314, 319 (G. Lucci). Oscar Savio, Rome: 163. Scala, Florence: jacket, 18–19, 24–25, 37, 42–43, 54, 55, 56–57, 58–59, 60, 62–63, 64, 65, 70, 71, 73, 74–75, 76, 77, 86–87, 88–89, 94, 95, 96, 97, 98–99, 100, 160, 164, 180–181, 189, 193, 197, 208, 210, 211, 212–213, 214, 215, 216, 217, 218–219, 220––221, 222, 223, 234–235, 240–241, 244, 245, 251, 265, 269. Henri Stierlin, Geneva: 34, 35, 129, 156, 157, 158, 194, 195. Victoria and Albert Museum, London: 233. Ole Voldbye, Copenhagen: 272. Woodmansterne Picture Library, Watford: 304, 306–307.

Acknowledgements

The publishers would like to thank the following people for their kind and invaluable editorial help:
Adriano Bocca, Albissola
Giorgio Cristoforidis, Salonika
Laura Gavioli, Ravenna
Adriana Miani, Milan
Christine Sevette, Milan

Agnoldomenico Pica would like to thank the following for their courteous assistance: Pier Maria Bardi, Museo d'Arte di San Paolo; Fortunato Bellonzi, Accademia Nazionale di San Luca, Rome; Carlo Bertelli, Lausanne University; Rosanna Bianchi Piccoli, Milan; Gianfranco Bustacchini, Accademia di Belle Arti, Ravenna; Carlo Fabrizio Carli, Rome; Gianni Contessi, Trieste; Franco Girardi, Facoltà di Ingegneria della Sapienza, Rome; Riccardo Mariani, Geneva University; Bruno Miorin, Scuola Mosaicisti del Friuli, Spilimbergo; Giovanni Quadrella, Rome; Joseph Rickwert, London; Alex Wall, Architectural Association, London; Viviana Terkuc, Salviati & C., Venice.